Lipsology

the art and science of reading lip prints

Lipsology

the art and science of
reading lip prints

Jilly Eddy

Lipsologist

BOOK PUBLISHERS NETWORK

Book Publishers Network
P.O. Box 2256
Bothell • WA • 98041
Ph • 425-483-3040
www.bookpublishersnetwork.com

Visit my website: www.lipsology.com

10 9 8 7 6 5 4 3 2
Printed in the United States of America

ISBN 978-1-940598-09-3
LCCN 2013953014

Editor, Graphic Design: Keri Detore
Editors: Ann Morris, Julie Scandora, Diane Faria
Indexer: Judy Dunlop
Cover designer: Laura Zugzda
Typographer: Stephanie Martindale and Leigh Faulkner

Disclaimer: This book is designed to provide information on lip print reading for the reader's enjoyment and self-knowledge. It is sold with the understanding that the author is not engaged in rendering legal, accounting, medical, or other professional services. If legal or other expert assistance is required, the services of a competent professional should be sought.

The purpose of this manual is to educate and entertain. The author shall have neither liability nor responsibility to any person or entity with respect to any loss or damage caused, or alleged to have been caused, directly or indirectly, by the information contained in this book.

DEDICATION

To my mom, Geraldine Swigart, and dad, Robert Swigart, who were always willing to put on lipstick and kiss paper for me. First, they did it for the fun, then to hear what their lip prints had to say about them, and, always, to help me with my ongoing research. I thank them for having been so supportive of my Lipsology adventures!

ACKNOWLEDGMENTS

A big thank you to all my family and friends (and all the lovely casual acquaintances—strangers before I read their lip prints) who have made lip prints, giving me the gift of your informative kisses that will last forever. You know who you are, and I appreciate and love you all very much for being supportive and encouraging me to write my Lipsology books.

I would like to thank especially Keri Detore for the excellent work she has done in designing and editing my first book, which I use to train people to be Professional Certified Lipsologists, *Lipsology: The Art and Science of Reading Lip Prints, A Training Manual.* Much of the work she did for me in that book (which is available only in conjunction with my professional certification course), I have used in this book. She has edited and entered information, designed the layout, and changed things more times than anyone would have dreamt would be wanted or needed. I bless her and appreciate how her work has played a big part in my ability to share Lipsology with others!

Credit and appreciation also go to Ann Morris for her exceptional editorial contributions and willingness to get things done in a timely manner. Thank you to Judy Dunlop for her belief in my work and her extremely valuable skills in indexing my book. Thank you to Sheryn Hara, Julie Scandora, Laura Zugzda, Stephanie Martindale, and Leigh Faulkner for pulling my book together into published reality. What an amazing team you are.

And my heartfelt thanks go to Diane Faria for being my project manager, computer consultant, and enthusiastic beginning lipsologist in training, having fun collecting and reading lip prints by the book, without me by her side. Her feedback and help were critical in helping me determine how to make this book easy to understand and useful for people I can't coach in person.

Also, I extend a special thanks to my students who gave feedback to make me a better teacher. Thank you for your questions and interest and dedication to learning something new. Thank you for using what I taught you about lip prints to make a positive difference in the lives of others. I am very proud of you all!

Most important, I want to express my sincere gratitude to Marsha Kremen, the love of my life, for her continued support, love, and encouragement throughout this long process. I thank her for the hugs and kisses (including her precious lip prints on encouraging notes), the reminders to get up and step away from the computer (stretch a little, get a drink of water), finding the important Lipsology files I had accidentally lost or deleted, and saving my sanity in all sorts of ways.

Thank you, sweetheart!

PREFACE

Lip prints can talk! My name is Jilly, and I understand their language. I call my system of reading lip prints Lipsology, and I am delighted to share it with you.

Every time I go to work, I put on my cherry-red suit, black tie with multi-colored lip prints (think blue, red, hot pink). Off I go, happy as a clam—I am an entertainer. I read people's lip prints.

Yes, you heard me right—people put lipstick on and kiss paper for me. Then I tell them all kinds of things, based on their lip print's size, shape, fullness, color, lack of color, spacing, corners, and special markings. This information describes their characteristics, energy levels, emotional and health issues, and special messages their lips have for them. Their lip prints reveal the personality they have carried for years, as well as issues they may be dealing with now. People are amazed and intrigued at how accurate their readings are.

It is a great conversation starter and ice breaker. Not only do people have fun; they also learn something meaningful and have something interesting to talk about with other guests. "Hey, what do your lips say about you?" "I'm the Cheerleader!" "I'm, the Go-To Person!" "I'm the Juggler!" "I need a Hug!"

I developed my Lipsology system of reading lip prints by studying thousands of lip prints and relating their shapes and special markings to the personalities and conditions of the kisser. This is an art and science that I continue to study and develop. I have been using Lipsology to entertain at private and corporate events for over twenty years. My clients include Microsoft, Nordstrom, Neiman Marcus, and even the United States Navy.

I also teach others to be Certified Lipsologists. They are all wonderful, strongly intuitive, talented people. I am proud of how well they use my Lipsology system to enrich the lives of so many people. But we cannot be everywhere—we can teach only a limited number of people in person. Not everyone wants to be a professional entertainer.

However, many are interested in learning Lipsology for their own enjoyment and enlightenment. People ask me all the time, "How did you learn this?" "Where did it come from?" "How do I learn?" "Is there a book?"

So, dear reader, here it is finally. I know some of you have waited a very long time. Thank you for your patience. Please use this book for your own personal growth and discoveries. Share what you learn with others. Have fun using Lipsology to make a positive difference in the world.

CONTENTS

PART I: INTRODUCTION

WELCOME TO LIPSOLOGY

There is a wealth of knowledge in your lip prints. They reveal your personality and more, including special messages you need to hear. Your lip prints, like a chapter of a book, tell your story and reveal answers to an astounding variety of questions. Are you creative and artistic? Do you need a vacation? Do you have champagne and caviar tastes?

You only need to put on lipstick and kiss paper to start your lip print reading adventures.

In fact, before you proceed any further, get lipstick, apply it to your lips, and kiss a piece of paper in whatever way suits you. Then print your name (because we do not like loose, unidentified lips) and the date (the date is important because it reminds you of what was going on with you when you made them).

Now take a good look at what you see, and compare your lip prints to the map below. These are just a few of the marks you will learn about ...

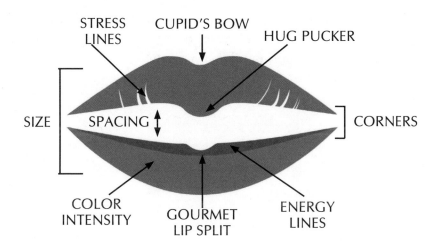

Of course, to know how to decode all this information and accurately read lip prints, you will need to study and practice the information contained in this book. But for now, you could skip ahead and take a peek ... I won't tell ...

This beginner's guide includes the history and development of Lipsology, as well as easy-to-understand information of what the shape, size, color intensity, corners, spacing, fullness, and special markings have to say about you and to you. Most of the more than one hundred categories and subcategories are included here, each with examples of individual diagrams and actual lip prints.

Each chapter also includes extraordinary personal anecdotes, which show how giving and receiving lip prints can open up a whole new world of interaction and intimacy, which people are craving. You will find Lipsology is fun, informative, and amazingly accurate.

I can tell you that once you read even one chapter of this book, you will find yourself staring at people's lips. You will wonder what their lip prints will look like on paper (on a cheek, a napkin, a coaster, the back of a business card), and you will want them to put lipstick on and kiss paper for you. They will be intrigued by what you are doing, and they will want to kiss paper for you so you can read them like a book!

So, have fun collecting lip prints and learning how to read them. Soon you will be using your new lip print reading skills to communicate with others in a uniquely different, caring, and playful way. Go ahead—use this knowledge to be the life of the party reading your friends' and family's lip prints!

A BRIEF HISTORY OF LIPSOLOGY

In 1981, I purchased a book of celebrity lip prints titled, *With Love From … A Collection of Celebrity Lipographs*. Little did I know that purchase would start me on my fascinating journey of collecting, identifying, and interpreting lip prints. I displayed it on my coffee table and loved looking at all the stars' prints.

One day, I opened it to look at Mick Jagger's lip prints, only to find that my brother had added his own lip imprint with a note stating that his lips were as good as Mick's! Soon all my visitors were putting their lip prints in that book, along with a witty remark or special note.

When that book was filled, I purchased a blank book and continued collecting lip prints, like others who collect autographs, in what I called my "Kiss Books." These lip prints were mostly those of family and friends, people I knew very well. I also found that lip print collecting was a great way to meet new people. Just let others know that you think they have beautiful lips and that you would like to have their lip prints, and most of the time, they are happy to give them to you.

For several years, I ran a private limousine service with a black 1967 Fleetwood Cadillac limousine. The car was rumored to have been owned by Tony Curtis, and some customers were celebrities. The company name was Lips Limo, and all passengers paid in dollars and lip prints.

By 1990, I had collected thousands of prints and was interviewed by the *Chicago Tribune* about my collection. This generated further media attention, and I was contacted by the *Johnny Carson Show*. As the producers of the show pointed out, the lip prints were not really expressing anything, and they asked the fateful question, "Jilly, can you tell something based on his lip prints?"

Do Our Lip Prints Really Have Anything to Say?

I decided it was time to find the real answer to this key question. I began by researching other personality-reading arts, such as Chinese face reading, palmistry (hand analysis), astrology, graphology (handwriting analysis), numerology, and Tarot cards. I read books, took classes, and talked with practitioners of these subjects. I wanted to know what was involved in how these arts revealed information. I discovered that they all utilized some form of symbols and markers in combination with using a system that interpreted what they saw to reveal useful information about a person's character, personality, energy, emotions, and health.

Then I got busy studying my giant collection of lip prints. Fortunately, as I mentioned before, most of my prints are of family and friends, people I know well. Looking carefully at each lip print, I began to see distinctive patterns of sizes, shapes, and special marks. I sorted them, based on what I identified in one person's lip print and saw in another; ones with the same size or patterns were grouped together. But what did they mean?

I looked and asked and sorted and listened ... After I completed the sorting, I had to determine their significance or meaning. My identifications and interpretations were based on a combination of what seemed a possible fit from my studies of other "ologies," my intuition, and my analysis of what the lip prints were reflecting back to me and whether or not it made sense to me.

For example, I equated a print of large lips with a person who likes to do things BIG, likes to do them right, does not like to be rushed, and likes to finish what he or she starts. Small lips mean the person is very detail oriented, well organized, and good at keeping a project on time and under budget. Dark color lip prints, which come from heavy pressure of the lips on the paper, translate as extremely strong energy, show that the person takes good care of himself or herself, has leadership qualities, and can get things done. Light color lip prints, which come from a light pressure of the lips on the paper, equal a very low energy, tired to the point of exhaustion, and a need to take the time to recharge the battery.

After I decided what I thought something could mean, I then would tell my interpretation to the family members or friends who had that particular marking in their lip prints. They would say, "Yes, that is true about me, but you already know that about me." I would say, "Yes, but I am saying it because of this mark I have identified in your lip prints."

Next I figured out what to name the categories. Some were simple and made sense right away, like the size or shape categories. Others just came to me, because of an association with a shape or an activity, such as Cupid's Bows, Gerbil Wheels, and Hug Puckers.

To further my research, I had my mother and several other family members and friends send me lip prints of their hairdressers, dentists, girlfriends, teachers, co-workers, and florists—all people I did not know. I would read those lip prints with the understanding they would report back where I was right or wrong. When I repeatedly reached 80 to 100 percent accuracy, the art and science of reading lip prints was born.

I coined the terms "Lipsology" and "lipsologist" in 1996. I have made presentations to a variety of organizations, including the International Behavioral and Medical Biometrics Society. And since 2004, I have been teaching others to use my lip-reading system to become Certified Lipsologists.

I continue to collect, identify, and interpret thousands of lip prints every year. When reading a lip print, I look for over one hundred marks. Now when I identify something in a lip print that I have never seen before, I have an extensive knowledge base to help me decide what this new mark could mean. I then decide what to name it and in which category or subcategory it belongs. I repeat the process of testing my theory to make sure it qualifies as a new mark!

You Don't Have to Be an Entertainer

For over two decades, I have used Lipsology to entertain professionally at corporate and private events. I have found Lipsology to be a fun and satisfying way of interacting with others. I use my lip print reading skills and sense of humor to entertain, inform, encourage, and empower. Lipsology has taken me to exciting places I would never have gone and introduced me to wonderful people I would never have met, while providing me with a sustainable source of income. It opens doors and brings joy and enlightenment to myself and others.

You do not have to be a professional entertainer for Lipsology to play a meaningful role in your life. Just knowing about it allows you to learn to use it for yourself and with friends and family members. Let's get started …

HOW LIPSOLOGY WORKS

Much like practitioners of palmistry, handwriting analysis, and face reading, lipsologists read a part of the body, the lips—frozen in time with a lipsticky lip print—in order to discover and describe aspects of a person's being: how they function, what needs attention, and how they can benefit from this knowledge. Since your lip prints vary, depending on emotional and physical feelings and daily life, and because these situational effects are reflected in lip prints, you can make and read them often for up-to-date information.

But keep in mind it is the print of the lips that reflects back to you all the information, NOT your physical lips! You cannot look at a person's mouth and know for sure how it will look as a print of lips. You can guess and may be right sometimes. More often than not, you will be wrong. You must have the person's lip prints for an accurate reading!

Lipsology Is Light and Fun, but It Also Has a Serious Side

While reading lip prints is entertaining, equally important is that our lives are enriched by using this information to help ourselves and others. Following is an example of the emotional impact and beneficial communication that can take place during a lip print reading:

I was entertaining at an event where many of the guests were curious to hear each other's readings. The first reading was for a young woman of about twenty-five who seemed very confident and sophisticated. I discreetly asked her if it was all right to discuss some sensitive issues revealed in her lip prints. She said it was as these people were close family and friends. So I continued her reading.

First, I noticed her extreme Hug Pucker, which suggested she needed more hugs, emotional support, and affection from family and friends. After I explained the indicator, the people around her leaned in closer and gave her a group hug. She blinked back tears.

Next were the Stress Lines showing in her upper lip, indicating she had some tremendous stresses in her life right now that she might not be managing all that well, issues that she did not have much control over.

I also saw a Gale Mark, which reflects a loss or separation from a loved one and suggests that the person is going through a very difficult time. She started sobbing. I put my arm around her and explained that her lip prints wanted her to remember that both time and the love of family and friends help us get through difficult situations.

Another guest later told me that the young woman's mother had recently passed away. The family presumed that she was adjusting to her loss and did not need any help. Because of the information revealed through her lip print reading, it became apparent that she really did need some support and that they would make sure she got it.

As this story shows, lip prints are reflections of individuals and situations at the moment in time that the lip prints are made, offering lip print makers a chance to see themselves more clearly and the opportunity for others to understand them better.

Just Collecting Lip Prints Is Meaningful

You can have fun, as I did, with just asking loved ones to take the time to put on lipstick, make lip prints for you, and personalize them with a quick note and/or fun artwork. You will be creating a scrapbook of good times and lasting memories. Any time you want, you can look at those old lip prints and be reminded of the time and place and occasion they commemorated. The following story from one of my students illustrates how even just collecting lip prints, without reading them, can make a significant difference in people's lives.

My elderly mother suffered a stroke about ten years ago. For many years, my father took care of her at home. He was finally forced to place her in a nursing home.

Over the years, her capacity for communication has diminished, and recently she has even stopped talking.

During a recent family gathering, I mentioned my new venture—Lipsology. My mother was present in her wheelchair, but her gaze was focused down at her lap. I explained the philosophy of Lipsology and asked for everybody's lip print. The first to give me a print was my older brother, Ray. He has a heavy beard and needed to use the little mirror I provided to find his lips. As he delicately applied lipstick, my mother suddenly looked up at him. Her eyes widened, and her face lit up with surprise. She actually smiled a real smile and started laughing. The stroke affected her facial muscles, and she usually never displayed a real smile. We were all so surprised and delighted that she noticed the oddity of my brother applying lipstick, and we all had a great laugh.

That evening, I received prints from everybody, including my mother, who wanted to take part. I put the lipstick on her and held the paper up to her lips. Then it was time for my dad to give me his prints, but he said no, he wasn't going to put on any lipstick. He's old and stubborn. Well, I asked my mother if she would like Dad to put lipstick on and give me a lip print, and she looked up at him and said strongly, yes. So, of course my dad, the old softie, caved in and gave me his lip print. We had a wonderful time that evening, and the lip prints provided so much entertainment.

For this student, her family's reactions and the resurgence of her mother's long-lost smile created a valuable memory for her of her mom's heart being touched as no other words or events had done. The simple act of having her family members make lip prints brought the family together in a way that none of them could have imagined. To further the significance of this story, this student's mom and sister have both passed away. She still has their lip prints, which are even more meaningful to her now.

THE TRUE SPIRIT OF LIPSOLOGY

Using Lipsology lets you put people in the limelight. By focusing just on them, in a kind and loving way, you give them time to play and be silly. In addition, Lipsology readings provide something meaningful and personal to think and talk about.

Lipsology not only is a tool to learn about yourself, it also helps bring people closer together. These days, personal interaction with others seems more limited than ever, and we are separated in many ways. Many are lonely, too busy, and not sure about how to meet others, or maybe they are afraid. People are staying home to work because of traffic or job loss, and kids sit at their computers rather than play with each other. People walk down the street talking on their cell phones instead of personally speaking to each other! But there is something warm and friendly and informative about giving and receiving and reading lip prints. They are intimate and tangible.

You never know what the highlight of a reading will be. You may be going through changes, and your lip print reading gives you assurance you are on the right path. You may need a break from a hectic life, and even though you and your mom just talked about that very thing yesterday, only after seeing your Ghost Lips, do you finally get the message to slow down. Maybe, the reading affirms something you have been thinking about doing, and you are happy to see that revealed in your lip prints.

A good example happened at a graduation-night party. I read the lip prints of a young lady, and I told her that her lip prints said she enjoys food and could be a gourmet cook. She was delighted and hugged and thanked me. With a high five, she smiled and said, "Yes, right on! In fact I'm going to culinary school next year!" She also told me she was relieved that her lip prints revealed she had made a good choice.

The true spirit of Lipsology is to give people a form of entertainment that sparks a twinkle in their eye, moves them to giggle, laugh out loud, blink back tears, or have a good cry. It surprises them with wonderful, unexpected experiences and amazing insights, and gives affirmations that warm their hearts and stimulate their imaginations.

PART II: LEARNING AND USING LIPSOLOGY

THE BASICS

Now that you have had a taste of Lipsology, I am excited for you to collect lip prints and learn all the different lip print marks and their meanings. But first I would like to cover the basics of how my system works. We'll start with needed equipment for collecting lip prints, followed by guidelines for successfully collecting, identifying and interpreting lip prints.

Equipment

Besides lips and lipstick and something to make lip prints on, the following items are useful for making, collecting, and reading lip prints.

Equipment Used Most Frequently

Lips – yours or someone else's

Lipstick – dark, bright colors are best

Paper – high quality, smooth, plain, white paper or cardstock (non-glossy), or a spiral notebook of the same

Pen – to sign and date lip prints and jot down pertinent information

Equipment Used Less Frequently

Mirror – some people like to use one while they are applying lipstick

Kleenex – for removing lipstick

Magnifying glass – the better to see fine details

Ruler – lip print size matters; a ruler helps to measure until you have a better assessment of size

Carrying case – can be a bag or binder; something to keep your supplies and lip print collection in

Plastic sheet protectors – good way to store lip prints

Now that you have the right materials and understand how to use them, you are ready to start collecting as many lip prints as you can. Remember, the more the merrier!

COLLECTING LIP PRINTS

It is a good idea to start your collection with your own lip prints. Next are family, friends, and colleagues—people whose habits, personalities, and energy levels you are familiar with and, ideally, people who are willing to discuss what is going on with them at the time. You can jot down a few lines about how you and/or they are feeling and what is going on in your lives. For example:

Do you have any aches or pains?

What is your energy level?

How busy are you?

Are you celebrating any major accomplishments?

You can review this information later, after you have learned how to read their lip prints. Their responses will help you build your confidence as you see that your readings are a strong match for their situation.

Respect people's decisions. Some people may not want to give you their prints. Do not be concerned because, for every one who does not, there are a hundred more who do.

Let people make lip prints the way they want. There is no right or wrong way to make lip prints. Whatever way anyone wants to do it is the right way. And DO NOT COACH others in how to make their lip prints. Let them make their own decision about how to apply the lipstick and kiss paper to make their lip prints.

Collecting lip prints is simple. Just ask your subjects to:

- **Apply lipstick**

- **Make one or two lip prints** – Limit the number in the beginning to simplify your identifications and interpretations. (Later you will be able to handle more lip prints.)

- **Number the order in which the lip prints were made** – It is important to do this when making multiple prints at the same time.

- **Date them** – Lip prints change, depending on circumstances, and the date helps you both remember what was going on with the person when he or she made the prints.

- **Print their name clearly** – You do not want to end up with unidentified lip prints.

- **Indicate which way is up** – An upside-down lip print can give you a completely incorrect reading. If in doubt, ask the person to use arrows to indicate which way is correct.

- **Make notes of pertinent information you have obtained from each subject** – Later, these notes will give you valuable affirmations of the accuracy of your interpretations.

The more lip prints you get the better. Your own lip prints, combined with those of your family and friends, will provide a wonderful basis for learning how to identify and understand lip prints.

Express gratitude. Whether or not you are reading the prints, always thank people for giving you their lip prints.

IDENTIFYING LIP PRINTS

To receive and/or give an accurate reading, you need to see clearly the lip prints you are looking at. Always use good lighting and, if possible, have a magnifying glass handy. Correctly identifying what you see will ensure an accurate reading.

The following points are important to keep in mind when you are identifying each lip print.

Original lip prints are preferred to copied, scanned, emailed, or faxed lip prints!

Do not make assumptions. You cannot tell how people's lips are going to print by looking at their mouth size or shape. A big six-foot guy with a large mouth can have small lip prints. Kids can have lip prints as large as adults' prints, and adults can have lip prints as small as children's.

You cannot tell the following from lip prints: age, gender, race, religion, or ethnicity.

Lip prints from the same person do vary. The impressions they make on the paper depend on how they are feeling, where they are, who they are with, and what their circumstances are at that time. What shows up in a person's lip print determines what is supposed to be discussed. An accurate reading will convey what the person's body, mind, and spirit want him or her to think about or act upon.

Lip prints reveal only a partial picture of the person. If a characteristic does not show, it does not mean the person does not have that characteristic. It may not be important at that time. Or other issues or characteristics may dominate. For whatever reason, some traits may just not be revealed at the time.

Certain marks do not necessarily have an opposite meaning. For example, when two lip prints, made at the same time, have the same spacing between the upper and lower lip, it means you can trust that person. If one has close spacing and the other wide, it does not mean you cannot trust that person. It reveals something totally different. (See "Spacing, Two Prints: Space Increases," page 120)

Some lip print traits can contradict each other. For example, if you are looking at size and one lip print is large and one is small, they may seem to contradict each other. However, the message is that the person can operate one way or the other, depending on what he or she is doing or wants to accomplish.

When considering a category, such as Shape of lip prints, and looking at different lip prints by one person, share the meaning of each. For example, if you are in the Shape category and one lip print is triangle-shaped and one is square, the information revealed by each is part of this person's reading and adds layers to what you know about the person.

When looking at a single lip print that first looks one way and then another, read about both. Perhaps the shape at first appears oval, but as you stare at it, it looks like a diamond; it morphs on you. When you cannot decide, read all options that seem possible.

Accept the lip prints for what they reveal; do not excuse them away. Sometimes, people may not like how their lip prints look. They may tell you that their lip prints are dark or pale because of the color of lipstick they used, how heavy they put it on, or how much pressure they used when they pressed their lips to paper. Or they may say the lipstick kind of smeared all over their face and that is why their lip print looks so weird. At this point, you, as the lip print reader, need to explain to them that all these things contributed to what their lip prints look like and reflect what their lip prints want to talk about. If they are ready to listen to you, more likely than not, they will find your reading amazing and even a little scary because of how accurately their lip prints reveal what was important for them to hear and act on.

If you are not sure and/or do not know what something means, just say so. First of all, you are just learning and may not have read all the different categories. Second, even if you have, most people cannot remember all of them without lots of practice. Third, you may be looking at a brand new mark, one that is not identified in the book. (Identifying new markings is covered in detail in my training manual and Certification Course. See "How to Become a Certified Lipsologist," page 153.)

Lipsology lets you show people specifically what their lip prints are saying. It is not just staring at someone's lip prints and saying anything that comes to you. You will be able to say to a person, "See here in your lip print," pointing out what you are looking at. "This is what reflects the meaning I am able to share with you." The messages are FROM them TO them, and you are the interpreter.

INTERPRETING LIP PRINTS

Even though you can just jump right into a category and see what it says and then switch to another, it can be very helpful first to learn each category and subcategory in the order presented. This will also help you to know what is available in each category so you do not miss something.

In the beginning, I believe you will have more fun and easily understand my system if you systematically learn to identify and interpret each category, starting with size, shape, color intensity, energy lines, stress lines, and fullness, etc. Some categories, like size and shape, are identifiable in everyone's lip prints; others are special markings that can come and go or may never show up at all. Similar to handwriting, no two lip prints are identical—even from the same person. This is because there are endless types of sizes, shapes, formations, angles, etc., which will be discussed in detail. The approach of this book is to analyze specific parts of each lip print and explain each marking in order to compare it to the overall print and other prints.

Start with just one lip print at a time, one category at a time. As you go through each category, you will find generic and real-life examples to help you identify which subcategories best match your lip print. Once you identify them, you will be ready to read the interpretations. It is helpful to jot down brief notes of each mark that you observe and its meaning. If you made two or more lip prints, repeat the process for each lip print. And when two or more lip prints look very similar, this resemblance emphasizes the given messages.

After you have mastered each category, you can start each lip reading by making note of what jumps out at you first. What is your first impression? What caught your attention? Is it the size or a special marking, for example, or a large indentation in the center of the inside edge of your lower lip? Usually, what most impresses you at the start will be the most important thing for you to consider. So start with that trait and see what it reveals. Then pick the next trait that jumps out at you and repeat the process as your time allows. As you practice, you will begin to see how there are layers of information, which you can weave together to tell your story.

Some Interpretations Involve Sensitive Issues

When you are reading your own lip prints, be prepared to see traits that indicate you are not taking as good care of yourself as your lip prints would like. Perhaps your lip prints are light in color, reflecting back to you that your energy is low. The message is to remind you that you need to rest! Or you may have Stress Lines that say something is draining energy from you. You know we all have worries and stress, but when these stress lines show up in your print, it offers an opportunity for you to think and talk about what is going on in your life that needs your attention. It offers you suggestions about what could be helpful to you, such as figuring out what you can do differently so you do not feel that energy drain.

When reading for others, keep in mind people's need for privacy. It is very important when you see sensitive information in other people's lip prints, for example, Stress Lines or Gale Marks, that you pay close attention to whether it is okay to talk about it. Depending on the occasion, the situation, and even the place, it may not be appropriate to address the issue at that time. The best time is usually when you are alone with the person. If in doubt, ask the person if it is okay to talk about some sensitive issues shown in their lip prints. When giving anyone a reading, do your best to accurately assess the person and the situation. Be thoughtful, kind, and respectful of the person's feelings. Sometimes, the best thing you can do is offer to give people a hug! And let them know you are happy to talk with them later if they would like.

You Create Magic

Magic happens for you and the people you share your Lipsology knowledge with. You may have all stepped out of your comfort zone and are glad you did. That magic results when those people you are interacting with trust you and are willing to be playful and try something new. It can be as much fun for you as it is for them. By reading with kindness and humor, you will get a chance, if only for a little while, to touch other people's hearts.

People's lip prints are unique and informative and a wonderful souvenir of the moment. Sometimes you can ask people to put their lip prints on their refrigerator until they do what their lip prints suggested. They may talk for a very long time about what their lip prints had to say about them and to them and how their lip print reading made them feel special. And they will want to get together with you and do it again sometime because Lipsology is fun!

LIP MAP

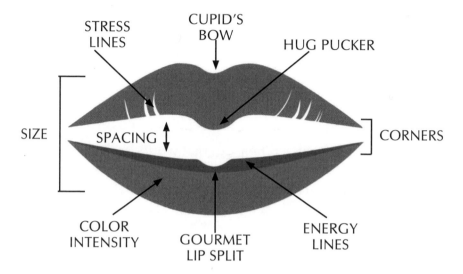

STRESS LINES

CUPID'S BOW

HUG PUCKER

SIZE

SPACING

CORNERS

COLOR INTENSITY

GOURMET LIP SPLIT

ENERGY LINES

Though there are many more categories and subcategories than shown in this map, these are the major categories and as much as can be labeled clearly on one diagram. Some are identifiable in everyone's lip prints; others come and go or may never show up. As you compare the characteristics in the map to a lip print, you will decide if the lip print has the feature or not. You will determine to what degree the characteristics are distinct and extreme, average or slight, totally missing, or somewhere in between.

As mentioned before, it is best if you are familiar with all the marks. Work to understand each individual trait because both showing and missing traits can have different and significant interpretations.

Say you decided that if a mark is not showing in your lip print you will not look it up. That can be a big mistake for some categories, such as the Hug Pucker or Cupid's Bow. For example, one of the most common features of a person's lip prints is to have no Cupid's Bow (listed as "NONE"). This means that the person does not like to be told what to do. While it is true that most of us do not like to be told what to do, what is amazing is that this characteristic is showing up in your lip prints! And you cannot assume that having one means you like to be told what to do. Depending on its configuration, it means something entirely different. (See "Cupid's Bow on Upper Lip," page 69.)

Before we get started with the individual categories, it is important for you to understand the significance of the upper and lower lip.

Upper and Lower Lips

Upper Lip

People's upper lips reflect their external world, their public side. This includes how others perceive them, how they react to events, how they interact with others, and how emotional and affectionate they are. Injury or trauma to a person's upper body (from the waist to the top of the head) can also be revealed here.

Lower Lip

People's lower lips reflect their internal world, their private side. This includes their feelings, sense of humor, eating preferences, health issues, and their notions of sentiment and romance. Injury or trauma to a person's lower body (from the waist to the bottom of the feet) can also be shown here.

PART III: PRINT MARKINGS AND INTERPRETATIONS

OVERVIEW

When you first begin reading lip prints, be patient with yourself and recognize that it may take a while to learn the markings and their variations. Also, Lipsology includes a layering aspect and depth that can only be learned with experience. Take your time and remember to have fun.

This section takes you through each of the categories listed below, along with their subcategories, including generic examples, real lip print examples, detailed interpretations, pertinent notes, and stories.

Size

Shape

Color Intensity

Energy Lines

Stress Lines

Fullness

Cupid's Bow on Upper Lip

Cupid's Bow on Lower Lip

Hug Pucker on Upper Lip

Hug Pucker on Lower Lip

Gourmet Lip Split

Corners

Spacing

Special Markings on Upper Lip

Special Markings on Lower Lip

Position of Prints on Paper

SIZE

Lip size demonstrates how a person tackles projects.

To determine a lip print's size, eyeball it, using these depictions as a guide. You can also measure if you like. Part of determining the size has to do with your intuitive perception. Pay attention to your first impression.

Sometimes a lip print will seem to fit somewhere between two sizes. Likely the meanings of both apply. This is also true when you have multiple lip prints that are different sizes. Both descriptions will contribute to an accurate reading.

large
w 2¼″ – 3″, h 1½″ – 3″

medium
w 1¾″ – 2¼″, h 7/8″ – 1¾ "

small
w 1″ – 1¾″, h ¾″ – 11/16 "

SIZE

These people like to do things big, and they like to do things right with the right tools. They do not like others nitpicking about how much the project is going to cost or when they should complete it. They do not like to be rushed—they go for high quality over fast turnaround. They like to finish what they start and do it right—or not do it at all. (I entertained for a Microsoft event where some of the guys there said, "We call it, 'Go big or go home!'") If they cannot have free rein, they usually do not want to play!

SIZE

These people are "Jugglers." Balance of work, play, children, relationships, and schooling is important to them. They have mastered the ability to handle multiple projects at a time with seeming ease. But they have a tendency to beat themselves up when everything is not going as smoothly as they would like. They need to acknowledge they are doing a great job, choose to focus on what is going well, take credit for their accomplishments, and ask for help when they need it. They would be wise not to take on any more projects at this time. Knowing when to say "no" is as important as knowing when to say "yes."

SIZE

These people are detail oriented, well organized, and work hard to finish their projects on time and under budget. They are a master at work that requires attention to minute details and meticulous results. They are good with facts and figures; it is important to them that the facts and figures are accurate because their decisions are based on them. They do not take anything for granted: they study the steps necessary to meet their goals, and then, only after careful consideration, they move ahead.

SHAPE

Shape indicates how successful a person is and in what ways. Shape also reveals aspects of how easy the person is to get along with and how he or she deals with conflict.

Shape has to do with the outside perimeter of the lip print—the overall impression without including the Cupid's Bows or Pushing Bars (the indentations or protrusions seen on the upper and lower lips, in the center of the outer edges) or indentations on the corners of the lip prints.

Exception to this is the wavy lip print. In this case, do consider every indentation and/or protrusion on the outer edges.

Even though you decide on the shape with the above instructions in mind, sometimes a single print will morph on you—for example, what originally looks like a diamond then appears to be an oval. In such a case, both may apply, so read both descriptions to get more information about the subject.

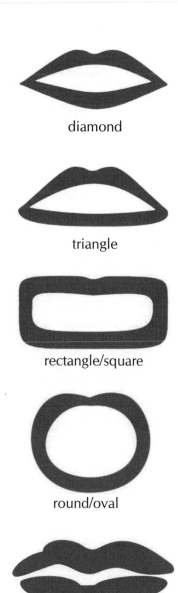

diamond

triangle

rectangle/square

round/oval

wavy

SHAPE

Diamonds are a girl's (and guy's) best friend, and so are people with diamond-shaped lips! They sparkle and shine.

Whatever they do, they do it very well. They are very successful, competent, and accomplished; whether it is their career, going to school, or in their home life, they do a great job from which they receive wonderful satisfaction. They are wonderful mentors, generous with their time, and committed to serving their community.

Also note they have all the qualities of the person with triangular-shaped lip prints.

I found the perfect example of this when I was at a writers conference. At a break before the next class, I headed to the bathroom where a long line of women were waiting. Several of them were talking about how I read lip prints so I offered to do quick readings. The next thing I knew I had a line of my own. I heard someone behind me say, "You should do this too." Another voice responded, "Okay."

I turned and grabbed the next person's card, looked at her lip prints, then extended my hand, and said, "Congratulations!" She said, "What for?" I responded, "Because you have diamond-shaped lip prints, and that tells me you are a very successful person—extremely competent and accomplished in all that you do—and you are very well known for what you do …"

Laughter and a few squeals of "Oh my God!" came from the crowd. In defense of my interpretation, I said, "Well, I don't know what is so funny; that's what her lip prints reveal. Also, that she is a mentor and helps others to be successful."

During all this, my thumb had been covering the lady's signature on the card. Finally, I moved my thumb and read "Jean Auel"—the author of the *The Clan of the Cave Bear* and the keynote speaker for that evening. I looked up and grinned. "Aren't I good?"

She was grinning too. And she said, "Yes! I like this! Can I have your business card?"

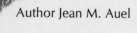

Author Jean M. Auel

SHAPE

From a solid base, these people point others in the right direction. Often working behind the scenes, they help others achieve their goals and dreams. They have a unique ability to recognize and cultivate human strengths and talents. Their vision and support helps others overcome their challenges and succeed on their own. They get along with others easily. They are natural "Talent Scouts" and could be a personal or athletic coach or in human resources. Whether they get paid for their services or not, they can help others by articulating what they think others would be good at doing and encouraging them to try it.

SHAPE

RECTANGLE/SQUARE

Like a brick or a heavy stone, these people are firmly planted and not easily knocked over. They are very well-grounded in their beliefs and know what they will and will not do. Males with this shape of lip print are referred to as "Godfathers" and females as "Godmothers" because of their solid positions in their family and community. If someone needs advice, muscle, or even money, that person is the "Go-To Person." These people are respected for their guidance, clarity, and direction.

SHAPE
ROUND/OVAL

Usually the shape looks round or oval with no rough edges. But if you *do* see a blunt or sharp protrusion, called a "Zinger," coming from one or both corners of the print, there is an unexpected contradiction in the interpretation.

Round with no Zingers: These people like things to run smoothly; they dislike conflict, controversy, or confusion. They like to work cooperatively with others and they will bend over backwards to see the other person's point of view. They look out for others and want everyone to be happy. These "Patters" give nice little pats on the back and ask, "How can I help?"

Round with Zingers

Round with Zingers: These people like things to go smoothly, and do not like to fight or argue. However, they have the ability to verbally nail people to the wall, or at least speak their minds when needed. (See "Zingers" in "Corners" section, page 110.)

SHAPE

Wavy shape lip prints have lots of curves, dips, and dives and definitely can include Cupid's Bow or Pushing Bars, but it also has to have more than just those markings.

Wavy lines on both the upper and lower lips indicate the person is an artist of some kind; he or she possesses a lot of creative talent and a vivid imagination. These people are versatile in their ideas, tastes, and abilities. They are actively using their talents and proud of their work. Also, their talent is known and appreciated by others.

They usually get along well with others (although they can be temperamental sometimes), and many of them like being the center of attention.

When people have wavy lips and say they do not think of themselves as artists, their lip prints are suggesting they put some energy into an artistic activity because it is likely they would be good at it and the activity would add balance to their lives.

Not having wavy lip prints does not mean the person is not artistic! He or she may be the most artistic person in the world, but at this time it is not being revealed. And of course, maybe the person is not artistic at all. But do not assume one way or the other.

COLOR INTENSITY

Color intensity reflects a person's outward and reserve energy.

Multiple lip prints from one subject with different color intensity tell a story about how the person's energy changes. Do not assume the first lip print is always going to be the darkest. It is important for the lip prints to be numbered in the order they were made because the story differs depending not only on the look of the print but also on the order each lip print was made and the location of each on the paper. You will learn more about this later in the "Position of Prints on Paper" section (pages 141–149).

dark color upper and lower

medium color upper and lower

light color upper and lower

upper lighter color than lower

upper darker color than lower

mottled upper and lower

COLOR INTENSITY

Outward and reserve energies are strong. This person is the "Cheerleader," the "rah, rah" person! These people have lots of energy, and others know it. They take excellent care of themselves. Once they decide what they want to do, there should be no reason why they cannot succeed. They use their joy and enthusiasm to accomplish their desires. They have excellent leadership qualities and are good at getting others to buy into their ideas. They could, sometime in their life, own their own business, be on a board of directors, or at least have others working for them.

COLOR INTENSITY

Outward and reserve energies are average. They know when to rest and are steadily active, productive, and reliable. Balance among work, play, school, and family is important to them, and they can handle them all for a while, but not forever. Sometimes their energy or time runs out. They need to decide what is most important to them and put their energy there first.

COLOR INTENSITY

LIGHT COLOR UPPER AND LOWER

Outward and reserve energies are low. I call these "Ghost Lips." These people's lip prints are reflecting back to them that they need some time to themselves without concerns for anyone else's issues. They need to take as good care of themselves as they do everyone else. They need to take time to meditate and recharge their battery and discover what it is like not to be exhausted. To this end, it is recommended that sometime soon they go on a little restful holiday—away from home, three days minimum, no electronics, no hidden agendas, by themselves! And they need to put their lip prints (as a reminder) on their refrigerator until they go.

LIP STORY

Once I did a reading for a young lady at a Seattle Design Center party. She was beautiful and smartly dressed, but her lip prints were all washed out and ghostly looking. She gave me her lip prints and said she hoped I could see them enough to read them, that she must not have pressed hard enough or used a dark-enough color, and that she really did not like how they looked.

She looked great, but her lip prints told me that she was exhausted, spread thin, stressed out, and in need of a relaxing spa holiday. I told her this, and she looked amazed and said I was "right on!" She went on to explain that she was raising three kids (as a single parent), going to school full time, and working full time. And she really did not feel like taking the time and energy to put more lipstick on and kiss the paper again!

COLOR INTENSITY

UPPER LIGHTER COLOR THAN LOWER

Outward energy is low, reserve strong. Others have to push these people to do things; they are the first ones wanting to quit or go home. They never seem to have enough energy to do the things someone else wants them to do. Yet, if it is their own idea and something they really want to do, they have plenty of energy. Their upper lip is suggesting it would be nice if they work on resting more often so they have enough energy to enthusiastically help others, as well as do what they want to do.

COLOR INTENSITY

Outward energy is strong, reserve low. Everybody thinks these people can jump, run, dance, and sing—just go on forever—and that is what these people want others to think. They use so much energy helping others and overdoing some things that there is not much left in reserve. Their lower lip is warning them to take some time for themselves; a rest is needed.

COLOR INTENSITY

MOTTLED UPPER AND LOWER

Outward and reserve energies fluctuate. These prints have a combination of light and dark color showing in each lip. The light color = tired; the dark color = peppy. These people have energy, and then they do not, and it repeats; they have energy, and then they do not, and so on. They have a tendency to go, go, go, like the Energizer Bunny, until they crash!

This is not a good sign, especially if the lip prints are more light than dark. To operate on a more even keel, these people would be wise, when others ask them to add more to their already full plate, actually to weigh "yes" versus "no" instead of immediately saying "yes," which they have a tendency to do. These two sentences may be very helpful to them: "I need to think about it. I'll get back to you."

ENERGY LINES

Energy Lines are dark lines located on the outer and inner edges of the upper and lower lips. Energy Lines also may appear in the lip corners (see "Information Funnels with Energy Lines" in "Corners" on page 109).

Energy Lines indicate where and how strongly a person's energies are focused.

dark line upper outer edge

dark line lower outer edge

dark lines upper and lower outer edges

dark line upper inner edge

dark line lower inner edge

dark lines upper and lower inner edges

ENERGY LINES

These people put lots of energy into whatever they are doing. This could be their career, a relationship, school work, or maybe a special project. Others are aware of their plans and how hard they are working toward achieving their goals.

ENERGY LINES

Others are not aware of the extreme amount of energy this person is channeling into his or her private matters—maybe even secretly. This could be a career change, caring for a loved one, writing a book, or a spiritual discovery—something the person feels he or she has to handle alone. These people should ask for assistance if they need it— they might be surprised by who would help.

ENERGY LINES

DARK LINES UPPER AND LOWER OUTER EDGES

These dark lines look as if you took a marking pen and completely outlined the outer edge of both the upper and lower lip. I call them "Mr. or Ms. Stretch Marks" because they remind me of a rubber band. These people are putting lots of energy into whatever they are doing. They are very busy doing things that others are aware of, and they are also busy doing things that others are not aware of. Their plates are very full; they are stretched to the max. It is important that they do not take on any more projects at this time.

When you see Mr. or Ms. Stretch Marks, it can be very helpful for you to say and do this: Write down the word "Normally." Then say it slowly. Remember not too fast. It helps to practice in front of a mirror, saying it very slowly with conviction. The rest of it goes like this: "NOOOORMALLY, I would be glad to help you. But right now, I am not allowed to take on more at this time." Notice I did not ask you to say no. First of all, you are not good at saying it, and second, people are not used to hearing you say it. But saying "Normally, I would ...," gives you some breathing room and time to take care of all the things you are already committed to.

Do not let someone give you a hard time over this. We do not want that stretched-out rubber band to snap! So take care of yourself and remember to say: "Normally ..."

ENERGY LINES

This line indicates guarded emotions. People with this mark have a protective shield up and do not show their true emotions unless they are sure they will not be misunderstood. Others have to prove themselves to these people; only after they really trust someone will they open up to another. People with this mark can be great poker players!

ENERGY LINES

This line implies the person is protective of his or her feelings. These people's feelings are easily hurt; they like to wait until they know someone well before getting close to him or her. It is a good idea for them to look out for themselves, but also try not to be too sensitive to others' comments or actions. They need to get all the facts and remember not to jump to conclusions before they decide what is going on with others.

ENERGY LINES

These lines reveal that a person can be extremely difficult to get close to. It shows a protective energy surrounding both their emotions and feelings. Others have to prove themselves to this person; but once they do, this person is the best friend they ever had. People with these lines probably have friends they made long ago. These are "Keepers"—people who reciprocate exceptional kindness and friendship.

It also has another meaning. Look closely and see a "Lip Print within a Lip Print"—a unique and lucky sign that says these people are almost always blessed with an extra boost of energy when they need it. But be aware that, if this coloring fades or becomes mottled, it says they are misusing this gift and they need a rest, even though they may not realize it.

Lip Print within a Lip Print

STRESS LINES

Stress Lines are white lines that come in several different configurations. Stress Lines indicate drained energy and that a person is dealing with stress and difficult or disappointing situations. These lines may be vertical or horizontal, they may go all the way through the lip print or end partway, and they may be on the upper lip or the lower lip or both.

Carefully study and understand the descriptions in this section because not all white lines are stress related.

When you see Stress Lines in your lip prints, always be gentle with yourself and be open to thinking about your situation in a different way. See this as an opportunity to listen to what your prints are telling you and make some changes.

When you see these lines in someone else's lip prints, always be kind and thoughtful. Since these marks can indicate very sensitive issues, it is wise to assess the situation and make sure it is appropriate to discuss them. Is the person in some setting where he or she might not feel comfortable talking about sad or stressful things going on in his or her life? Sometimes it is good to point out the Stress Lines and actually ask the person for permission before

vertical white lines on upper inner edge

vertical white lines on lower inner edge

vertical white lines on upper and lower inner edges

Gale Mark: vertical white line or lines through upper or lower lip

STRESS LINES

discussing out loud. You can also ask the person if they would like a hug, or at least consider saying something comforting. Pay close attention to the individual's response and proceed accordingly.

For another stress indicator mark, check the example in "Stress Lines in Hug Pucker" on page 87.

horizontal white line across upper lip

horizontal white line across lower lip

STRESS LINES

VERTICAL WHITE LINES ON UPPER INNER EDGE

These vertical white lines start on the inside edge of the upper lip and end within the body of the lip and appear to drain into the space between the upper and lower lip.

These print markings reveal an outward worrier dealing with people or events that the person has limited control over. Since he or she may be unable to fix these things, the key is to figure out what he or she can do differently to feel less physically tired and emotionally drained. These lip prints say they need to look out for themselves in a kind and loving way. Stress-reducing suggestions for them are: 1) talk to someone they trust and make a plan for what they are going to do

differently, 2) do it, 3) let go of hesitation (trust themselves), and 4) do not try to fix everything. Making changes in a caring and/or professional way, without worrying about everyone else, allows them to regain control and to feel better and more energetic.

STRESS LINES

VERTICAL WHITE LINES ON LOWER INNER EDGE

These vertical white lines start on the inside edge of the lower lip and end within the body of the lip.

These lines indicate an inner worrier. Others see these people as carefree, but the truth is they privately rehash things that are bothering them, and this can be an energy drain. Also, the Stress Lines on their lower lip have to do with their private life, things they have some control over. They need to decide what they can do differently so they do not feel so stressed. They should follow the same stress-reducing steps as discussed on the preceding page, do their best, and go forward! They will feel better and have more energy.

STRESS LINES

These vertical white lines start on the inner edges of both the upper and lower lips and end within the body of the lips.

Totally stressed, these people are definitely the worriers in the group. Their friends and family are aware of this and love them anyway. Even though they fret over every little thing, they are endearingly protective and look out for others. They should try the previous stress-reducing suggestions (see "Vertical White Lines on Upper Inner Edge" on page 57).

STRESS LINES

The Gale Mark is a white line that goes all the way through the upper and/or lower lip, with a look that the lip is entirely split in two (or more) sections.

People with Gale Marks are living in a difficult situation and/or have experienced a loss or separation from a loved one. Regardless of where the Gale Mark is on people's lips, their lip prints want to remind them that time and the love and support of family and friends and whatever they believe in are helping them weather their gale storm. And like a gale storm that can cause havoc and destruction, it does not last forever, and when it is over, there is renewed growth and strength.

STRESS LINES

This line indicates that something or someone disappointed this person, or things just did not work out the way he or she wanted them to. The main message for people with this mark is for them to ask themselves, "What did I learn?" and "What can I do differently next time so I don't feel this way?"

STRESS LINES

People with this mark in their lip prints are disappointed with themselves somehow. There is something they did not do exactly right or to the best of their ability or something they did not do and wish they had done. The message here is to learn from the situation and take this time to grow, not beat themselves up.

FULLNESS

Lip fullness shows how expressive people are verbally, their listening and writing skills, and their social ability. Fullness, or lack of it, also indicates a person's thoroughness, frugality, and analytical and mathematical skills.

upper lip full,
lower lip full

When the upper lip is the same fullness as the lower lip and they are symmetrical, these people have excellent communication skills: listening, speaking, and writing. And whatever they know, they know it well enough to teach others.

upper lip thin,
lower lip thin

For each lip print you read, you will first decide individually on the fullness of the upper lip and read that information. Then do the same thing for the lower lip. Obviously if the lips are the same fullness, you are done. But if the fullness is a combination, first read the information about the upper lip and then follow with the lower lip. Also remember to read the combination information ... Good Luck!

upper lip average,
lower lip average

combination: upper lip fuller
than lower lip

combination: upper lip
thinner than lower lip

FULLNESS

UPPER LIP FULL, LOWER LIP FULL

Upper Lip: This person is an excellent listener and problem solver with whom people like to share their difficulties and issues. These people are good at getting others to follow their vision. They make good project managers and delegators.

Lower Lip: This person is very socially oriented and generous with others, sometimes to a fault. Children and pets adore these people, and they could be nannies or animal trainers. They like working with others and sharing what they know. They definitely like to talk! They have excellent verbal and/or written skills. They could be writers, speakers, or entertainers. And if they are not doing any of these things, their lip prints are suggesting they try putting some energy into one. They will be pleasantly surprised at how good they are at it.

FULLNESS

Upper Lip: These people are picky perfectionists! Well-organized and detail-oriented, they are also good at thinking outside the box to find new, more efficient ways of doing things. They are good researchers and marketing specialists.

Lower Lip: These people are very analytical and excellent with numbers or statistics—things that have to be exacting. Hard workers, frugal, and economical, they like to be productive and efficient. They can be better at sticking to a budget than others and are logical and self-controlled. They make excellent engineers, scientists, bankers, history teachers, architects, financial planners, accountants, realtors, and CEOs.

FULLNESS

Upper Lip: These people are good listeners. They work well alone or with others and are not particularly picky. They will do a good job, but things do not have to be perfect.

Lower Lip: These people are good with numbers and the bottom line without being obsessive. They like things to be well balanced but do not worry if they are not. They have good communication skills and will be on time and do their part without much supervision.

FULLNESS

This combination says that, even though these people are excellent listeners and problem solvers, they do not like to listen for very long. Do not tell them the same thing five different ways—they got it the first time! Also do not waste their time with long explanations; get to the point. They want to help make a plan and get on with it. They know more about others than others know about them. They think things over and choose their words carefully. They could be psychologists, doctors, lawyers, human resource personnel, consultants, nurses, bartenders, or hairdressers.

FULLNESS

People with this combination may not always listen as well as others would like them to. They may be thinking about what they want to do or say or are distracted by new ideas; they can be so into their own thoughts that they really do not know what was said. Though they may have been told something or requested to do something, they do not remember it because they are so distracted by their own thoughts. It is important for this person to make eye contact, write things down, and be reminded of what needs to be done. The ability to concentrate on their own thoughts makes them excellent scientists and inventors.

CUPID'S BOW ON UPPER LIP

The V-shaped indentation on the center outer edge of the upper lip is the Cupid's Bow shape we see when we look at a person's mouth. But, not everyone has this shape and, even if one does, often it doesn't print that way. In the extreme V shape, the Cupid's Bow resembles the bow Cupid uses to shoot his love arrows. In Roman mythology, Cupid is the god of love, and his name means "to desire." While this shape in the extreme signifies, among many other things, a strong desire to make a positive impression, just as our desires change, so does the Cupid's Bow shape.

The different configurations of the Cupid's Bow reveal a person's temperament and interactions with others. It also suggests how goal-oriented the person is and how concerned he or she is about making an impression.

A single lip print may have many layers of information in this area. You may see an extreme indentation and an underlying straight line (which is the "None" category) and maybe a gray area that is pushing up. This is complicated, beyond our study in this book, so for now stay focused on the strongest mark you see and read about that.

extreme

moderate/slight

energy line fades in
Cupid's Bow

Pushing Bar: center
protrusion up

CUPID'S BOW ON UPPER LIP

People with an extreme Cupid's Bow like to make a positive impression—they are concerned with appearances as well as interactions with others. They can go to a lot of trouble to leave a certain impression on others, such as seeking to make a favorable impression at a job interview by dressing for success or expressing themselves with extensive body piercing, elaborate tattoos, or wild outfits!

They look out for others, put a lot of energy into having good outcomes, but also like to receive appreciation and get positive feedback regarding their accomplishments. If they are not getting that feedback, they would benefit by asking for it and not waiting for others to be mind-readers.

They are attractive and charming and have a strong desire to increase the well-being of humanity. Although needs and demands of others play a significant role in their decision making, they can be manipulative. This shape also looks like a volcano. Stay on these people's good side—they have a temper! They may not show it often, but pushing them too long the wrong way may result in an intense emotional outburst.

My definition of an extreme Cupid's Bow is based partly on the personality of "Mr. GQ," whose lip print appears here. The maker of this lip print is a male fashion model, but he is also a construction worker. He always looks like Mr. GQ. His clothes are cool, his hair is styled, and even his fingernails are perfect. He likes to make a positive impression and goes to a lot of trouble to pull it off. He also looks out for others, but he has a temper—you do not want him mad at you.

Girl at the Bar's lip print here confirmed my definition and expanded it, helping me realize we each have our own idea of a positive impression. I was having dinner out with eight of my sister's friends in a midwestern steak house, and my sister asked me to read all their lip prints. While doing this, Girl at the Bar was watching us. She was smoking cigarettes, drinking beer, sported multiple tattoos and pierced body parts, and was wearing leathers and a tank top cut to her navel. She got her lipstick out, made that one lip print, and said, "Hey, I want to do this too." I took one look at that lip print, and I said, "Sure thing." She agreed that she liked to make an impression and did indeed have a temper.

Mr. GQ

Girl at the Bar

CUPID'S BOW ON UPPER LIP

These people are usually even tempered, cooperative, and versatile. They are excellent mediators and negotiators with a keen ability to see both sides of a situation; they make valuable assessments and help all come to a win-win position. Others' opinions moderately influence their physical appearance and actions, but they can get caught between what they think others desire and what they desire. This is especially true when two or more of their lip prints, on the same paper, have the exact moderate to slight Cupid's Bow shape. When this happens, their lip prints are saying that they would be wise to look out for themselves first, in a kind and loving way. If they do what others want them to do but do not really feel that it is best for them, it may be okay in the short term, but in the long run, it will not be good for anyone.

One reading I did was at a big Christmas employee party. The young man made three lip prints; all had exactly the same slight Cupid's Bow. I told him his lip prints said he was a good negotiator and mediator, but sometimes better for others than himself. He agreed.

I said, "Pay attention; there is going to be an important decision for you to make, and you may have others telling you what they want or think you should do. You would be wise to base your decision, in a kind and loving way, on what's right for you. If you say okay to make someone else happy or to get the person off your back, it may be fine for a little while, but in the long run, it is not going to work for anybody. Acknowledge the other person's needs and desires and explain that you really can't do it unless it feels right for you too." I explained to him that this was a message to him from himself. And I was merely interpreting what his lip prints were reflecting back to him.

Later, his mom, a lady for whom I often entertained, thanked me, although at the time, I had had no idea who her son was. He had gone home from that party mad at her—he was sure she had told me what to say to him. As it turns out, he had been engaged for two years, but he was resisting his girlfriend's pressure to get married; he had things he wanted to do that would not work in a marriage. His mom felt that the girl was not right for him. So he had assumed that she had asked me to talk him out of the marriage. In the end, after hearing what his lip prints had to say, he decided not to get married, and his mom said he is wonderfully happy—all because he listened to messages from his lip prints!

CUPID'S BOW ON UPPER LIP

These people do not like to be told what to do! They have their own style, their own way of doing things, and work to please themselves. They do not mind helping others but want only the details of what you would like them to do, including when you need it done, and then to be left alone to do the job. They are very good at figuring out the best way to do it. They do not like to be micromanaged.

They take good care of themselves. They work well alone but can also be a good team player. They are almost always even-tempered and are courageous and proud of their accomplishments.

CUPID'S BOW ON UPPER LIP

ENERGY LINE FADES IN CUPID'S BOW

These people are putting an extreme amount of energy into whatever they are doing, and others know it. They work hard towards their goals and want to please others. The problem is that they are not feeling appreciated—possibly in their job or relationship. The main message for the person is to do things differently. When things are out of balance, we need to look to ourselves to change. If it is the job, ask for some tangible form of appreciation: more money, sincere thanks, or fewer hours. If it is at home, ask for more help, more quality time together, etc. Figure out what is needed and how to get it. The other option is to move on. It is up to the person to take responsibility and make positive changes. When this is done successfully, the faded line will fill in.

CUPID'S BOW ON UPPER LIP

PUSHING BAR: CENTER PROTRUSION UP

The Pushing Bar is in the area of the Cupid's Bow and looks like a little mushroom pushing upward. People with this mark have high goals and high expectations. They push themselves and others in their area of influence (i.e., significant others, spouse, employees, siblings, friends, etc.) to be the best they can, setting the bar very high. Once they reach their goal, they immediately raise the bar without ever acknowledging how well they or others did. The harder they tend to push, the more extreme the Pushing Bar.

These people would be wise to take some time to bask in their glory, relax a little before starting work on another goal, and express appreciation to others for what they have done to get to where they are.

CUPID'S BOW ON LOWER LIP

There are two configurations of the Cupid's Bow seen on the outer edge in the center of a person's lower lip. One is a moderate to slight inverted V shape, and the other is a protrusion called a Pushing Bar because it is pushing downward.

moderate/slight

The Cupid's Bow on a person's lower lip reflects both how a person operates and achieves his or her goals and some things the person may not want others to know about them.

Pushing Bar: center protrusion down

CUPID'S BOW ON LOWER LIP

Seen most often on women's lip prints (but it certainly can be on men's or children's lip prints), this Cupid's Bow on their lower lip means they are operating in, or associating with, a stereotypical man's world. They have to come across as tough: speak with authority, make hard decisions, stand up to others, and call the shots. They can be more about getting things done than winning friends. The secret is that they really do have a softer side that they do not always show.

LIP STORY

I read for a lady who had a Cupid's Bow on her lower lip. After I told her what it meant, she revealed she was, indeed, the coach of her son's basketball team. She added, "If you're going to coach a high school boys' basketball team, you have to be in their face and act like a man. You have to be tough, accurate, walk the walk, talk the talk, and speak with authority. Otherwise you will not be effective."

CUPID'S BOW ON LOWER LIP

PUSHING BAR: CENTER PROTRUSION DOWN

People who have this protrusion, called a Pushing Bar, have very high private expectations, but others are not aware of them. In fact, others may think these people just fell into good times and things come easily to them. However, the truth is that they have worked very hard to get to where they are. Their lip prints are saying they need to celebrate their accomplishments and take a rest before setting another private goal.

HUG PUCKER ON UPPER LIP

The Hug Pucker is an oblong shape that looks like a little hotdog or mushroom. It can be located on the center inside edge of either the upper or the lower lip. Its name is associated with people's actions of showing affection by hugging and puckering up to give kisses.

extreme

On the upper lip, the Hug Pucker is located in the "area of affection." The oblong shape comes in all kinds of configurations, from extreme to hiding up inside the upper lip to even not showing. There can also be vertical white lines (Stress Lines) located in the area of the Hug Pucker that drain to the space between the upper and lower lip. These lines are not to be confused with the white lines that form the sides of the Hug Pucker (see "Recessive" example to the right).

moderate

slight

The Hug Pucker on the upper lip reveals information about the way people show affection, how much affection they want or need, and their ways of interacting and communicating with others.

recessive

Stress Lines in Hug Pucker

HUG PUCKER ON UPPER LIP

People with extreme Hug Puckers need a BIG HUG right now! For some reason, extra support and/or affection from family and friends would be greatly appreciated. Sometimes others are not aware of what is happening with this person but would gladly help if they knew. Lip prints of those with an extreme Hug Pucker say they may need to ask for some hugs or assistance and not expect others to be mind-readers. It is okay to ask for hugs.

When reading other people's lip prints and you see an extreme Hug Pucker, it may be beneficial to stop and give the person a big hug.

Little kids with extreme Hug Puckers may not be getting enough hugs and kisses. Pay attention and offer to give them a hug if they would like.

Lip print of
five-year-old
child

HUG PUCKER ON UPPER LIP

MODERATE

These people are wonderful "Teddy-Bear" huggers. Upon meeting or departing, they are generous with their hugs and can be counted on to be the first to hug and kiss others; usually they do this no matter where they are or the circumstances. In relationships, they want someone who likes to hold hands and hug, kiss and cuddle, and enjoy being physically affectionate.

HUG PUCKER ON UPPER LIP

SLIGHT

In public, these people are not going to be the ones to hug you first. They do like hugs from family or close friends, but do not expect them to initiate the hug. In a relationship, they really do not like someone hanging on them in public. In private, it is a different story; they are more spontaneous when alone with their partner.

HUG PUCKER ON UPPER LIP

When there is no Hug Pucker showing, there are two distinctly different
meanings. Half the people agree
to the first one as being accurate
for them, but the other half say it
is the second interpretation that is
correct for them. Read both interpretations and decide which best
describes you.

The first meaning is that these people are usually getting as many hugs
and kisses as they want and need.
They are good at letting others
know if they want more affection,
or they just go ahead and cuddle,
hold, and give hugs to others when
they feel like it.

Alternatively, they may not be getting enough hugs or kisses or
affection. This can be because they just are not interested for some
reason or because they are very busy and completely focused on
their career, a project, taking care of family, or some crisis. Whatever
the reasons, it could be beneficial for these people to be more aware
and work on being a little more spontaneous in showing affection,
especially if they are in a relationship or have children. Others may
very well appreciate the extra effort and attention.

HUG PUCKER ON UPPER LIP

These people can be moody! They can be openly affectionate one minute and then want to be left alone the next. This can be confusing to others, who may wonder if this person is mad at them. At times, they just need their own space, or they may want to be with only certain people.

Communication is very important; the message to people with the recessive Hug Pucker is to pay attention and figure out who would benefit from hearing from them (preferably in person). Though they may not be as openly affectionate or see someone as much as that person would like, it does not mean they do not love and appreciate all the other person does for them. After communicating, they will be amazed at how things ease for everyone.

HUG PUCKER ON UPPER LIP

These vertical white lines in the person's "area of affection" indicate stress is going on with the person's family or friends. Communication may be lacking, or disagreements or misunderstandings need to be resolved. Waiting for others to change or situations to resolve does not always work. These people need to figure out what they can do differently to eliminate any conflict or confusion, starting with being kind and considerate of others' needs and desires, while still looking out for themselves by taking control of what they can and getting help if they need it. Lastly, it is important to let go and move forward, rather than stand still and be a victim.

HUG PUCKER ON LOWER LIP

The only Hug Pucker seen on the center inside edge of the lower lip is an oblong shape that looks like a little hotdog or mushroom rising toward the upper lip.

moderate/slight

The Hug Pucker on the lower lip has to do with how people treat themselves and how confident they are.

HUG PUCKER ON LOWER LIP

These people have a tendency to give others recognition for accomplishments, but they are not good about acknowledging those things for themselves. They may also be looking to others for approval or some positive comment. They should be reminded that it does not matter what others know about their actions; what matters is that they know! It is important for these people to give themselves a big hug and a pat on the back for all that they have accomplished!

GOURMET LIP SPLIT

This V-shaped indentation is located on the inner edge of the center of the lower lip. This mark can look like a large karate chop or a slight indentation.

This mark reveals food preferences, sense of humor, and romantic or sentimental values.

When there are multiple lip prints with completely different Gourmet Lip Splits, share the information stated for all of them. Each one tells you more about the person and emphasizes how changeable he or she can be.

extreme

moderate/slight

different for multiple prints

GOURMET LIP SPLIT

These people are not cheap dates! They enjoy delicious foods and may be a gourmet cook or may live with someone who is. At the very least, they know the best places to go. They have champagne and caviar tastes. Someone who wants to take this person out for a special occasion needs to know the person has a very romantic side and appreciates four-star restaurants, soft candlelight, nice music, and all the things that create a romantic mood. They are extremely sentimental and good at remembering birthdays and special anniversaries. When involved with someone, it is very important to them that the other person remembers special occasions too.

These people are fun-loving and pleasure-seeking. They love the spotlight, being pampered and spoiled, and living in luxury. They would rather not have to work, but if they must work, it better be in attractive surroundings with interesting people!

They have a wonderful sense of humor and possess a delightful laugh that should be recorded so others can play it when they are not around.

GOURMET LIP SPLIT

These people enjoy food. When they go out to eat, they would rather go to a nice restaurant and not to a fast-food place. They prefer homemade meals to frozen dinners and enjoy having friends over for brunch or dinner parties. They are slightly romantic and sentimental. They have a good sense of humor and are fun to be with.

GOURMET LIP SPLIT

This usually means the person is not a stranger to peanut butter and fast foods. However, it does not mean these people are not good cooks (or that they do not enjoy the wonderful food their gourmet friends cook for them!). It may be that their gourmet leanings are just not being revealed at the time of this lip print making.

GOURMET LIP SPLIT

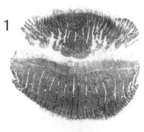

What if the person has made two lip prints at the same time, and one of them has a Gourmet Lip Split (GLS) and the other one does not? This sometimes means the person has all the characteristics that go with the GLS: loves food, can be a great cook, and has romantic and sentimental leanings and a wonderful sense of humor.

On the other hand, sometimes these people like to go to fast-food places (they may even "super-size"). They may forget a birthday and not laugh at jokes.

If they have shown a GLS in past lip prints, but not today, they may not be feeling well, or they may have lots of other things on their mind. The GLS is just not being revealed today.

CORNERS

Lip corners indicate how a person deals with change. They also indicate optimism, pessimism, happiness, or sadness. They may reveal a pack rat, or at least a collector, and how one processes or protects information.

Keep in mind lip print corners that are not noticeably turned up or down indicate the person is not overly happy or sad, respectively—or, at least, neither is being revealed. Consider them to be neutral.

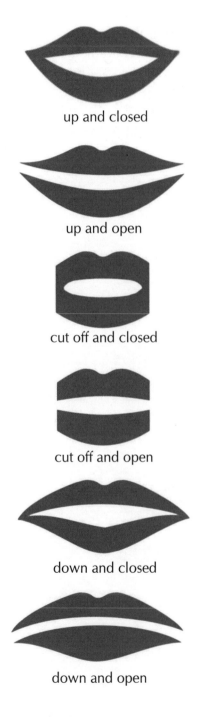

up and closed

up and open

cut off and closed

cut off and open

down and closed

down and open

CORNERS

Keep in mind that Information Funnels, Information Funnels with Energy Lines, Zingers, and Angel Wings may show on only one corner or both and they may be touching or not touching.

closed left side, open right side

closed right side, open left side

Information Funnels: V shape

Information Funnels with Energy Lines: V shape with dark lines

Zingers: blunt to sharp protrusion

Angel Wings: feathery protrusion

CORNERS

This indicates happy-go-lucky people. They are optimistic and used to things going their way. They are not looking for any major changes at this time, and major changes do not come easily to them. They do not like to be rushed when making a decision.

CORNERS

These people are happy and optimistic most of the time and do not like to be bored—they like to be busy all the time. They are multi-talented and have several things that they do equally well. Change comes more easily to people whose lip prints are not touching on the sides. Usually the wider the opening at the corners of their lip prints, the more open they are to accepting major changes.

CORNERS

These people are extremely focused on taking care of business. It is as if they have blinders on and may not be aware that others are concerned about them. They are trying hard to take care of many things—much of which are other people's wants and requests. Being so focused does not leave much time for any major changes at this time. Their lip prints want them to take some time in the near future to do something fun and silly, something they want to do just for the fun of it!

CORNERS

These people are doing their best to stay focused on taking care of business and going along with people and events. Although they do not usually rock the boat, they are wishing things were different. They are definitely ready for a change; the wider the opening, the quicker they want the change and the more they are actively participating in that change.

CORNERS

This print reflects people who are sad or upset at this time and could use a hug or a pat on the shoulder. They need to think positively. And even though they may not expect things to change quickly, their circumstances will improve.

CORNERS

These are the lip prints of people who are not happy campers. They need a hug or pat and some cheering up. Whatever it is that has made them sad or unhappy, they are ready for a change. Hopefully, they can see that moving along or taking a different direction will be beneficial.

CORNERS

This configuration can indicate that a person is holding onto the way things have always been and is aware of major changes coming up. It can also be the mark of a pack rat or someone who is a collector of things and/or information. In either case, these people do have a tendency to take things in and not let go of them. It could be that letting go of some things will help this person feel lighter.

I met Maddie, who was five years old, at her grandmother's birthday party. She was very talkative, interested in playing with my lipsticks, and made lots of prints using different colors on different Kiss Cards. She then listened attentively as I told her what her lip prints had to say about her. One of the things I said was that she was a pack rat of some kind. I asked her if she knew what that meant. She said no, and I explained that if she collected lots of things she could be considered a pack rat, but if it was only a few things she could be a collector; either way, there were some things she liked so much that she probably would have a hard time letting go of them. She thought for a minute and then said, "I do collect stuffed animals; mostly giraffes and monkeys. The other thing is I collect rocks. Mostly shiny stone rocks from the beach." "Yes," I said, "that would make you a collector."

Maddie's prints

CORNERS

This configuration has several meanings. It can indicate that the person may have been holding onto the ways things have always been and is wanting them to stay that way—possibly even reminiscing about the good old days. Similar to the configuration before this one, it also can be the mark of a pack rat or someone who is a collector of things and/or information. In either case, somehow things come in, and they do not go out! It could be that letting go of some things will help this person feel lighter.

CORNERS

These look like > or < and can be on one or both lip corners. If turned upright, it looks like a funnel. It signifies that this person needs lots of information to make a decision, especially one that involves a major change. If the corners are touching just behind the > or <, these people will be very slow to make a decision. They like to have plan A and B and maybe even C. Look closely to see how the Information Funnels are touching. The more they are touching, the longer and harder it will be for the person to make up his or her mind and take action. Be patient with such people. If the Information Funnels are not touching, these people will make their choice more quickly.

CORNERS

These Information Funnels are the same as in the preceding, but they have dark lines, called Energy Lines, on their inside edges. An individual with these marks knows confidential information and is very protective of it; others share things with such a person that they might not share with anyone else. The information needs to be accurate because decisions and counsel are based on it. Also, the person may have to really study information (more so than others) so they totally understand it.

CORNERS

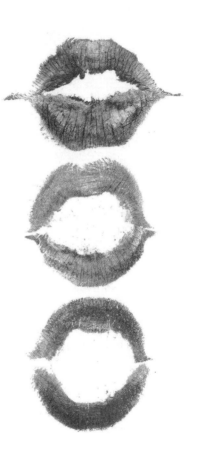

These are protrusions coming out of the corners of the lips and can be seen in all lip shapes (though quite unexpected when found on round/oval-shaped lip prints). They can be extreme and look like a sword or knife. People with extreme Zingers can nail others to the wall with their words. They can be brutally honest or just mean, not necessarily intentionally. The message for them is to try to think before they speak: be diplomatic when necessary and more forceful when necessary. They need to use good judgment.

Sometimes the Zingers are more subtle, coming from people who quietly and constructively point out what needs to be said without offending anyone. They are well known for speaking their minds. These people, such as lawyers and doctors, say things that others might not want to hear but that have to be said, nonetheless.

CORNERS

These can be subtle or amazingly they can look like a wing! They differ from Zingers in that they look more feathery. They belong to people whom others may already call angels. These people do kind, unexpected things for others. They are young or old, male or female, those whom others feel are gentle and helpful. They comfort others and make them smile. They radiate love.

In November 2004, I took a class on Chinese Face Reading at the Boeing Employees Parapsychology Club. At the end of the class, I mentioned that I collect and read lip prints. Everyone was quite interested to learn more. I gathered lip prints from several of the students and the teacher. The teacher's lip prints were quite unusual; they had a strange shape, especially on the left side that I had never seen. I pointed to it and asked her what she thought it could be or mean. She looked at it and with a big smile said, "It's my angel wing!"

A few weeks later in Portland, when I was entertaining at a holiday party, I saw a similar marking in a nine-year-old boy's lip prints. I explained what it meant, and the mother was amazed. She told me he is the sweetest, kindest soul she knew, that he is an angel, and that is what they have always called him!

Chinese Face Reading teacher's lip prints

SPACING

Spacing between the upper and lower lip indicates how open-minded or stubborn the person is. This spacing also reveals people's commitment to projects, how cautious or adventurous they are, and how honest and trustworthy they are.

The corners may be touching or open; the focus here is on how much space is between the inside edge of the upper and lower lip.

narrow

average

moderate

wide

SPACING

As mentioned before, you need to number your lip prints and ask others to do the same. This is especially important when reading multiple lip prints with increasing or decreasing space. Regardless of where on the paper the person has made the lip prints, start with the first one made. Starting with the second print will result in an incorrect reading.

For the purpose of this book, we are concerned with the comparison of just two prints made by the same person at the same time. (Spacing of three or more lip prints is complicated and covered in detail in the Lipsology Certification Course.)

two prints: space increases

two prints: space decreases

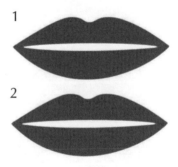

two prints: space consistent

SPACING

If the lips are touching each other or there is just a tiny bit of light showing, these people can be stubborn! They know what they want to do and how to do it. If they are going to be open to someone else's ideas or plans, that other person had better have a really good story.

These people can also be reserved observers and extremely cautious individuals. If they do not want to do something, all the reasoning in the world will not change their minds.

SPACING

NARROW

When there is a narrow opening, these people will listen to another's ideas, but if it is very narrow, they may just be pretending to listen. Their mind may already be made up, but they may give someone a chance to make a case.

These people are cautious and conservative and not apt to take uncalculated risks; however, they may be persuaded to try new things.

SPACING

Even though these people are not too wild and crazy, they do enjoy themselves! They tiptoe up and then jump in. They may not be the first to try new ideas, but they most certainly are not the last.

SPACING

These people are open-minded and easy going. They do not worry too much about things; they go along with others' plans and adjust where needed. They like to try new things and go to new places, though usually after researching them first. They like learning from others' experiences.

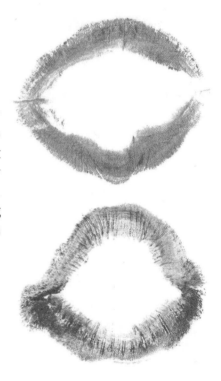

SPACING

These people are very open-minded and do not have preconceived ideas about people or situations. They like to hear all the information before they make up their minds. They leave the door open. And they want others to do the same. So rather than tell others what to do, these people let others learn from their own mistakes. These people like to be free of limitations, boundaries, and restrictions. They look forward to new ideas, tastes, sights, and sounds. Being extremely open-minded has its advantages and perils. Have fun, but be smart!

SPACING

These people are cautious at first and weigh their options before venturing too far. They open up more as their comfort zone is satisfied. If the space between the lips is just a little wider with each new print, these people are "Inchers." Their comfort level has to be satisfied with each move forward. If the space increases dramatically between the first and second lip print, they are very cautious at first, but once their comfort level is satisfied, they become gung-ho!

SPACING

1

2

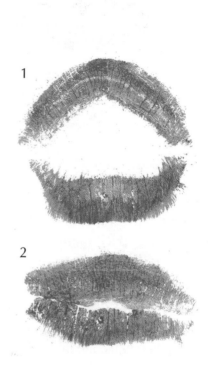

1

2

These people are initially open-minded and ready and willing to try new things. But after they get their feet wet, they have a change of heart, pull back, and may even stop altogether.

SPACING

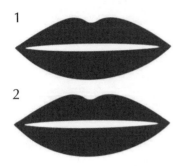

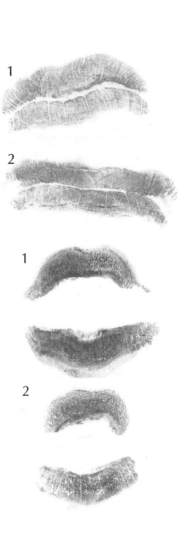

The space can be any width (narrow, average, etc.). The main criteria is that the space between the inner edges of the upper and lower lip is the same space (almost identical) for two lip prints that are made at the same time.

These people are consistent and honest. People trust them. They walk their walk and talk their talk. If they say they are going to do something or be somewhere at a certain time, others can believe them! They have high moral standards; when you have an agreement with them, their word is like a signature. If they do not want to try something, they have a reasonable explanation.

Keep in mind if someone does not have consistent spacing (that is, has increasing or decreasing spacing) it does not mean you cannot trust that person. Such lip prints have their own meaning with no relationship to trustworthiness (see the preceding two subcategories for information on what different spacing reveals about the person).

SPECIAL MARKINGS ON UPPER LIP

Though the markings on the upper and lower lips can look similar, they may or may not have similar meanings. Both their appearance and location are very important. Read carefully, and do not jump to any conclusions. It is a good idea to study all the "Special Markings on Upper Lip" section first so as not to be confused by jumping ahead to the Lower Lip section.

Unusual markings on people's upper lip reflect their external world: how others perceive them, how they react to events and interact with others, and how they receive messages of spiritual guidance or connections. Also trauma or injury to the upper body can be revealed here.

Angel Mark: V shape on outer edge

Emotional Marks: dark dots

Gerbil Wheels: scattered white lines

Injury/Trauma Mark: missing outer edge

Spiritual Lines: vertical white lines on outer edge

Starburst: white dot

SPECIAL MARKINGS ON UPPER LIP

ANGEL MARK: V SHAPE ON OUTER EDGE

Do not confuse this mark with the Cupid's Bow, which can also be a V shape indentation, but is located in the center of the outer edge of the upper lip (see Cupid's Bow Upper Lip, page 69).

The Angel Mark looks like a little V on the left or right outside edge of a person's upper lip. It indicates the presence of a guardian angel or guide on the person's shoulder. Usually there is just one, but sometimes there is one on the left and one on the right. It is a lucky mark to have! It says the person is being looked out for. Sometimes this strong connection is to a loved one who either is living far away or has died.

These angels are helping to create positive opportunities. The person's job is to pay attention and take advantage of his or her good fortune.

The Angel Mark also says that something may have happened to these people that would make one wonder why they are still here. The fact is, their angel or guide provided them protection because their time was not up and they have important things to accomplish.

LIP STORY

I read for a lady who had an Angel Mark and said, "You are right; I have this strong connection with my mom. She died several years ago, but she makes her presence known in the form of a ladybug. A month ago, I had to fly, and I hate flying. I was very nervous during take-off until I noticed a ladybug on the seat next to me. That was my mom reminding me everything was going to be all right."

SPECIAL MARKINGS ON UPPER LIP

EMOTIONAL MARKS: DARK DOTS

These dark dots look like black pepper or smudges that are scattered across a person's upper lip. They can be just a few spots or one big dot. The upper lip pertains to other people and events, and the marks indicate that something about one of these is bothering the person. The message for the person is to figure out the valuable lesson learned from the experience of dealing with the other person or event and how to move forward.

These people may also be emotionally holding something back that they would like to express to someone else. This mental strain is impeding their forward progress. By paying attention and figuring out what it is, they can work out a solution, and their lips will be soothed and smoothed!

SPECIAL MARKINGS ON UPPER LIP

GERBIL WHEELS: SCATTERED WHITE LINES

Gerbil Wheels are tiny, fine white lines, scattered on the body of the upper lip. The name comes from gerbils running constantly in their wheels, like what is going on in a person's brain—lots of thinking about what he or she must do.

To help you work more effectively and without so much strain, your lip prints are suggesting you do this short, easy exercise. In a quiet place where you will not be disturbed, get some paper and a pen. For each subject on your mind (home, school, job, etc.), starting with the one that is spinning the most in your mind, write down everything you want and need to do without any censoring. For each subject, prioritize the items on that list.

Then, pick two things from your list that you will ask others to help you get done. Next, pick two things to delegate. Understand that getting help is having others work with you, and delegating is having someone do the project without you. If you feel no one can do anything as well as you, write down exactly what you want someone to do, give a deadline, and say you will be giving feedback before signing off. This gives you some control. Finally, cross off two things that no one will notice if they are done or not.

With this more manageable list, as you complete a task, draw a heavy line through it. This reinforces that you have finished it and it can go from your brain. As your to-do list goes down, you will be more relaxed, have more energy, and have time for fun!

SPECIAL MARKINGS ON UPPER LIP

Usually, if you were to fold someone's lip prints in half, from left to right, they would be a close match. But when they are not, and it looks as if part of the person's lip print is missing on the outer edges of the upper lip, it reflects an imbalance, injury, or trauma to the upper part (above the waist) of the person's body. The area of discomfort is usually on the side corresponding to the missing part of the lip print. But sometimes, the person overcompensates with the non-injured side, and now it is not happy. Also sometimes the person is avoiding dealing with emotional issues; by focusing on the bodily pain the person is distracted from what is really bothering them. (Suggested reading is John Sarno's book, *Healing Back Pain*.) After these issues are resolved, the missing part of the lip print will fill in again!

The message to these people from their lip prints is to do something about it! Don't just suffer; consider visiting a medical professional. Look into strengthening exercises, maybe swimming. These people may have a tendency to put off doing anything until it gets worse, or they may get frustrated when they are not getting better as fast as they would like. Their lip prints recommend they try new things if the old ones are not helping them. Think outside the traditional medicine box and explore naturopathic or holistic treatments. And do not forget the power of positive thinking and visualization!

SPECIAL MARKINGS ON UPPER LIP

These are vertical white lines on the outside edge of the upper lip, indicating a strong spiritual connection to the universe. It is a guiding, healing force and a comfort to those with this mark. The energy force coming down to them is similar to the rays of sun that shine through clouds onto the water; some refer to them as the "Fingers of God."

Usually when Spiritual Lines are present, it is a sign of affirmation of the person's spiritual side, but sometimes it is a reminder that comfort and guidance is available to the person by awareness and cultivation of his or her spiritual side. Either way, it is a lucky sign to have in your lip prints.

Several years ago, I wrote to a well-known columnist that I enjoyed her articles and thanked her for her weekly valuable insights and words of wisdom. I explained what I do and asked her if I could have her lip prints for my collection, in return for a complimentary reading. She agreed and sent me her prints with a quick note that said, "Dear Jilly, Here you go – I'd be fascinated to hear what my lips say ..." She was amazed with her reading, especially hearing the meaning of her lip prints' Spiritual Lines. She said, "You are so right. I am extremely spiritually oriented and have been since birth. Even when I was little, I never felt I was alone. I knew I was being watched over and protected by a committee of angels." She gave me permission to use her lip prints, but asked that I not use her name since this was a private side of her that most people did not know about her.

Well-known Columnist

SPECIAL MARKINGS ON UPPER LIP

STARBURST: WHITE DOT

This is a white dot, "burst of light" or "positive energy." It has slight or no color and is a very special marking. The Starburst says these people radiate a brightness and positive energy wherever they go, lighting up a room with their presence, personality, and smile. They are usually optimistic and upbeat; people are attracted to them and happy to see them. Whether they are with their family or friends or co-workers, they are popular. Also, they may just be the "favorite" of one of their relatives!

SPECIAL MARKINGS ON LOWER LIP

Though the markings on the upper and lower lips can look similar, they may or may not have similar meanings. Both their appearance and location are very important. Read carefully, and do not jump to any conclusions. It is a good idea to study first the "Special Markings on Upper Lip" section so as not to be confused by jumping ahead to the markings in this section.

Special markings on people's lower lip reflect their internal world, their private side. This can include career and health concerns, indicate who has strong intuition, and suggest who would benefit from getting outside more. Also trauma or injury to the lower body can be revealed here.

Gerbil Wheels: scattered white lines

Health Marks: dark dots

Injury/Trauma Mark: missing outer edge

Mother Nature Lines: vertical white lines on outer edge

Old Soul or Gut Mark: inverted V shape on outer edge

Seeds of Change: white dots or small lines

SPECIAL MARKINGS ON LOWER LIP

GERBIL WHEELS: SCATTERED WHITE LINES

Gerbil Wheels are tiny, fine white lines scattered on the body of the lower lip. The name comes from gerbils running constantly in their wheels, like what is going on in a person's soul or gut—lots of mental activity about things he or she wants to do next.

To feel confident about the direction you should take, your lip prints suggest you do this simple exercise. In a quiet place where you will not be disturbed, get some paper and a pen to capture all the information running around in your brain, heart, and soul.

First, ask whatever/whomever you believe in for guidance. Then, without any censoring, write what you are passionate about. If you could do anything you wanted, with no concern for cost, time, or what others think, what would you love to do? Write freely until you cannot write anymore. Then, put away what you wrote for anywhere from a day to a month. Do not to read it right away. Setting it aside gives you breathing room to be open and ready for what you will be given.

When you feel relaxed and ready to read it, expect answers. Reorganize what you wrote into the small steps toward doing what you are passionate about! After you have rewritten the notes with those small steps, tear up the original writings and dispose of them, let go, and trust that your way will be made clear and the universe will happily assist you!

SPECIAL MARKINGS ON LOWER LIP

HEALTH MARKS: DARK DOTS

These look like dark dots, black pepper, or smudges that are scattered across a person's lower lip. They can be just a few spots or one big dot. They indicate a need for attention to health issues. The people with these marks are not taking as good care of themselves as they can. This may have to do with their thyroid, blood pressure, or hormones. It can be as simple as not drinking enough water or getting enough rest or exercise. They may know the issue. For example, the person who takes thyroid medication but has pepper in the lower lip print would be wise to have his or her thyroid checked. The person may be taking too much or not enough. Or someone with known high blood pressure may need to exercise more, etc. If the person does not know he or she has a medical problem, the lip prints, as in the following example, are suggesting the person find out and do something positive about it.

Barbara asked me if I would read her lip prints this particular evening. I had read her prints about eight months earlier (see Figure 1), which did not show the same Health Marks or Stress Marks as shown in the ones she made this evening.

Fig. 1. May 23, 2001

She did not tell me she was concerned about anything. She looked fine. But her lip prints told me she was not fine. Several things in her lip prints told a strong story about her energy and health. She had mottled, Ghost Lips with Gale Marks and Stress Lines, and lots of pepper on both her upper and lower lips, as shown in Figure 2.

Fig. 2. January 12, 2002

I gave her a hug and explained to her that her lip prints said she had a tendency to go like the Energizer Bunny till she dropped. She was exhausted, something was annoying her, and she was totally stressed and going through a difficult situation! Something was not right with her health, and she needed to do something about it. Also, I reminded her that the love of family and friends and time will help her through this difficult period.

She agreed and said she had not been feeling well, she had had an MRI and an ultrasound, and her doctors were running blood tests on her. On Monday, she would get the results. When she did, she called me and said they had discovered a blood clot in her left leg! They put her on medication right away, and she was feeling much better.

SPECIAL MARKINGS ON LOWER LIP

INJURY/TRAUMA MARK: MISSING OUTER EDGE

Usually if you were to fold someone's lip prints in half, from left to right, they would be a close match. But when they are not, and it looks as if part of the person's lip print is missing on the outer edges of the lower lip, it reflects an imbalance, injury, or trauma to the lower part (below the waist) of the person's body. The area of discomfort is usually on the side corresponding to the missing part of the lip print. But sometimes, the person overcompensates with the non-injured side, and now it is not happy. Also sometimes the person is avoiding dealing with emotional issues; by focusing on the bodily pain, the person is distracted from looking at the real issue. (Suggested reading is John Sarno's book, *Healing Back Pain*.) After these issues are resolved, the missing part of the lip print will fill in again!

The message to these people from their lip prints is to do something about it! Don't just suffer; consider visiting a medical professional. Look into strengthening exercises, maybe swimming. These people may have a tendency to put off doing anything until it gets worse, or they may get frustrated when they are not getting better as fast as they would like. Their lip prints recommend they try new things if the old ones are not helping them. Think outside the traditional medicine box and explore naturopathic or holistic treatments. And remember the power of positive thinking and visualization!

SPECIAL MARKINGS ON LOWER LIP

MOTHER NATURE LINES: VERTICAL WHITE LINES ON OUTER EDGE

These vertical white lines on the outside edge of a person's lower lip indicate the person needs to get outside for mental well-being and to stay in shape. A person can recharge his or her batteries by connecting with the beauty of nature and indulging the senses: look up at the beautiful sky, sit quietly and listen to the birds sing, and take time to touch and smell the roses. Equally important, the person needs to do some form of exercise outside, such as working in the garden, going for a hike, or getting someone to walk to a nearby park to play catch. He or she will benefit from the relaxation, the movement, and the vitamin D absorption (this absorption happens by being in the sun fifteen to twenty minutes without sunscreen, best accomplished before 10:00 a.m. or after 3:00 p.m.).

Also, these people have athletic ability and may already excel in sports. If not, they would be wise to figure out what they might enjoy doing and try it; they may be pleasantly surprised at how good they are and how their outdoor activity balances their indoor ones.

When I entertain at grad-night parties, I find that a significant number of high school graduates with Mother Nature Lines on their lower lip prints are varsity players!

SPECIAL MARKINGS ON LOWER LIP

OLD SOUL OR GUT MARK: INVERTED V SHAPE ON OUTER EDGE

Do not confuse this mark with the Cupid's Bow, which can also be an inverted V shape, but is located in the center of the outer edge of the lower lip (see Cupid's Bow Lower Lip, page 69).

The Old Soul Mark looks like a little inverted V on the left and/or right outside edge of a person's lower lip. It reveals that the person is highly intuitive. There are things these people know that they did not learn in school or read in a book; they just know, and they are almost always right. They may have a hard time explaining to others why what they say is true, but it just is, and others need to listen when they speak. This is a wonderful gift of true wisdom that they are to share with others. Those who receive such information may not understand its value at the time, but it will make a major, positive difference in a decision or path they take. Months or years later, they will say, "Thank you!"

This mark is also called a Gut Mark. The gift to those who have this mark is that they can trust their gut when making decisions. If their gut says no, they should say no or ask for more information or more time to study the information. The main thing is it has to feel right to be a good idea for them.

SPECIAL MARKINGS ON LOWER LIP

SEEDS OF CHANGE: WHITE DOTS OR SMALL LINES

Seeds of Change are white dots or small lines on the lower lip entirely surrounded by color, and they look like a seed or grain. People with these have an idea germinating. Or they may still be improving and nurturing it but are not done. Or they may still be trying to figure out what it is, or perhaps, they are not even aware of it yet. Whichever stage they are in, this mark is exciting to see and signifies that the person will be or is doing something important that will benefit many. The main message for these people is to affirm they are here to make a major difference helping others and they are on the right track. On the other hand, if they are not doing anything beneficial for others, this is a good time to figure out what they can do, and DO IT!

POSITION OF PRINTS ON PAPER

This section ties together in an intricate way all the bits and pieces you have been learning. Just as each lip print has many things to say, so too does the position of the lip print on the paper.

The paper is divided into columns and rows. Together, they define the zones on the paper. Paper position reflects relationships to timing, thinking, reality, and comfort levels.

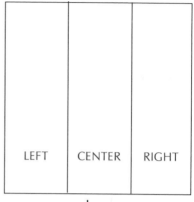

| LEFT | CENTER | RIGHT |

columns

Zones refer to a specific area on the paper where people have chosen to place their lip print. Imagine the paper divided into thirds horizontally and vertically, making nine distinct areas where they can put their lip print(s). The sequence in which they made their prints is also important. The order tells a story about what is most important to them and what path their journey is taking them on.

| TOP |
| MIDDLE |
| BOTTOM |

rows

Lip prints will not always fall into a specific column or row or zone but will sometimes overlap two or three sections. When that happens, read the descriptions of each area that the print inhabits.

TOP LEFT	TOP CENTER	TOP RIGHT
MIDDLE LEFT	MIDDLE CENTER	MIDDLE RIGHT
BOTTOM LEFT	BOTTOM CENTER	BOTTOM RIGHT

zones

POSITION OF PRINTS ON PAPER

COLUMNS: LEFT

 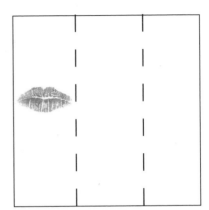

The left side of the paper concerns the past. Either the person is living in the past or concerned about the past. He or she may be stuck in the past or completely comfortable there. Multiple prints in the left column reinforce the focus on the past.

COLUMNS: CENTER

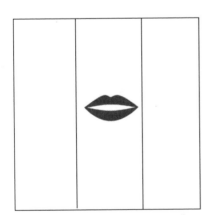 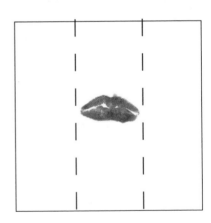

The center of the paper concerns the present. This person is focused on the here and now. He or she is not taking into consideration past experiences or concerns about the future. It is all about right now. It is all about today! Multiple prints in the center reinforce the person's focus on the present.

POSITION OF PRINTS ON PAPER

COLUMNS: RIGHT

 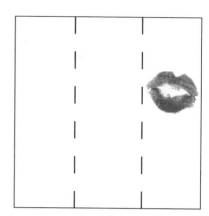

The right side of the paper concerns the future. This person is more concerned with his or her future than the past or today. Multiple prints in the right column reinforce the person's focus on the future.

Interpreting lip prints that appear in this right or "future" column is NOT about predicting the future. Rather, it is about the person being encouraged by, inspired by, or open to his or her lip prints' messages. This might mean changing behaviors or making decisions that will have a positive impact on the person's future. For example, when the person's lip prints are in the right column, and are light in color intensity, they indicate a lack of energy for future endeavors. He or she could choose actions to improve energy by resting more or not working as hard.

POSITION OF PRINTS ON PAPER

ROWS: TOP

The top horizontal row has to do with a person's thinking, dreaming, idea and goal planning, wishes, and challenges. Multiple prints in the top row emphasize the person's focus on thinking, planning, and dreaming.

ROWS: MIDDLE

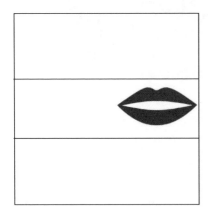 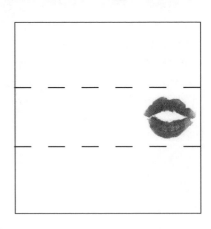

The placement of lip prints in the middle horizontal row deals with the reality of a person's daily activities: the doings and the actions taken at work, school, home, and play. Multiple prints in the middle row amplify the person's focus on reality.

POSITION OF PRINTS ON PAPER

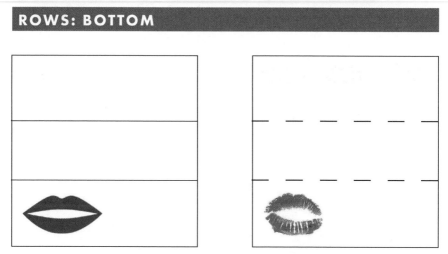

The bottom horizontal row has to do with people's comfort level. When their prints are down here, they are concerned with what makes them comfortable. They are either totally enjoying what they have or possibly feeling a need to make changes. It is also associated with material possessions. How much does the person need, and what can he or she let go of? Multiple prints in the bottom row emphasize the person's focus on comfort and possessions.

POSITION OF PRINTS ON PAPER

ZONES: TOP — LEFT, CENTER, AND RIGHT

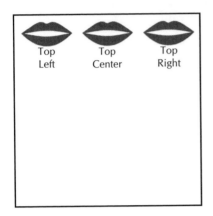

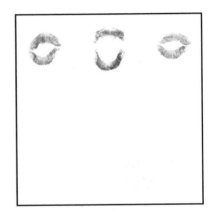

Zones: As mentioned earlier, lip prints will not always be placed exactly in an individual zone. When they overlap into different zones, read the descriptions of each area that the print inhabits. Also, keep in mind the location of the lip print tells you what the individual is focusing energy on, and the order the prints were made tells you what is most important to the person.

Top Left: The person has been thinking about past dreams, plans, and ideas; previous successes and accomplishments; or failures or mistakes. Reflection can be a good thing.

Top Center: This person is doing a lot of dreaming, thinking, planning, and maybe even some soul-searching about what he or she is doing or wants to stop or start doing, right now!

Top Right: This person's dreams, thoughts, and plans are for the future. Thinking ahead and setting goals help the person achieve his or her desires.

POSITION OF PRINTS ON PAPER

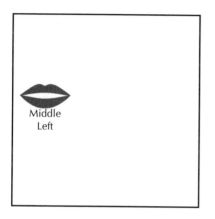

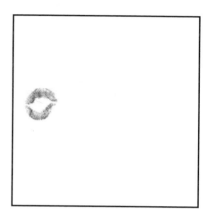

Middle Left: This zone concerns the past. These people may have been doing the same thing for a long time—living in the same place, going to the same school, or working at the same job. Or, perhaps, they've been hanging with the same friends or returning to the same vacation place year after year, instead of going somewhere new. Maybe they are happy and don't want to leave their comfort zones, or they are tired of doing the same old thing but are afraid of change, so they continue to stay with what is known. Whichever it is, positive or negative, their lip prints say they do have choices. They could choose to try something new. They might just like it!

Is the person perfectly content or in need of some kind of change? Look for clues in other parts of his or her lip prints.

POSITION OF PRINTS ON PAPER

ZONES: MIDDLE — CENTER AND RIGHT

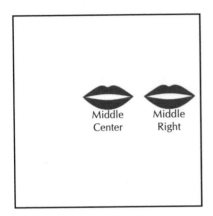

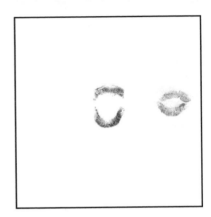

Middle Center: These people are living in the moment—the here and now—and dealing with whatever comes their way! What is most important for them to consider, learn from, and act upon today is reflected in the intricacies of their lip print.

Middle Right: Lip prints in this zone reflect what will happen if these people continue on the course they have set. By paying attention to their lip prints' messages, they can make wise decisions and continue successfully, or make adjustments where needed. For example, if someone makes a Ghost lip print in this zone, the message is for the person to pace himself or herself better and be careful of getting too tired.

POSITION OF PRINTS ON PAPER

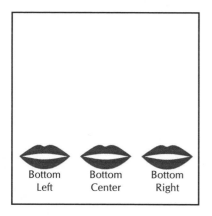

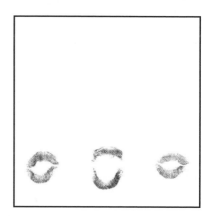

Bottom Left: These people's comfort level is tied in some way to their past. Whatever has worked for them before—and perhaps for a very long time—they continue to do. They are very comfortable with their old possessions, and they may resent anyone trying to upgrade them.

Bottom Center: Right here, right now, these people's creature comforts are important to them, as are their material possessions. Decisions to add to or change anything in these areas may have their attention.

Bottom Right: These people's future expectations include plenty of creature comforts: cozy home, safe surroundings, and nice possessions.

CONCLUSION

Now that you are familiar with my Lipsology methodology, I hope you are excited to give and receive lip prints and that you continue to enjoy sharing what you have learned about the language of our lip prints.

Make sure you have lipstick in your pocket, purse, or car. So, when you see a beautiful set of lips that peak your interest, you'll be prepared to ask, "May I please have your lip prints?"

Remember to take good care of your lips. Keep them in good shape because you never know when someone, somewhere, is going to walk up to you, lipstick in hand, with a big grin or maybe a shy smile, and ask you to kiss paper.

You want to be ready.

HOW TO BECOME A CERTIFIED LIPSOLOGIST

LIPSOLOGY CERTIFICATION TRAINING

We offer a Lipsology certification program that is an intensive and interactive course, designed to ensure high standards of Lipsology education and practice. The course is taught by Certified Lipsology teachers using a one-on-one approach, ensuring each student has personal guidance and support.

For more information on becoming a Certified Lipsologist, or to find a Certified Lipsologist in your area, please visit our website: www.lipsology.com.

GLOSSARY

Angel Mark Like a V shape on the left or right outer edge of the upper lip; shows that the person has one or more guardian angels looking out for him or her.

Angel Wings Located on the corners and can be on one or both sides; look feathery, like angel wings, and reveal a person who does kind, unexpected things for others.

Certified Lipsologist One who has successfully completed Jilly Eddy's Lipsology certification program.

Cheerleader Person whose lip prints are a solid, dark color, which reveals he or she has lots of energy and is good at getting others to buy into his or her ideas.

Color Intensity Due to the pressure applied in kissing the paper; reflects a person's outward and reserve energies.

Column One of three vertical positions on the paper where a person made his or her lip prints; left, center, and right representing past, present, and future, respectively.

Corners Where the upper and lower lips touch or do not touch, or appear cut off on the sides of the lip print; indicate a person's attitudes, how he or she deals with changes, information, and decision making.

Cupid's Bow, Lower Lip Located on the lower lip's center outer edge and can be anything from an inverted V to a pushing-down protrusion; reflects how a person operates and achieves goals.

Cupid's Bow, Upper Lip Located on the upper lip's center outer edge and can be anything from a V indentation to a pushing-up protrusion; indicates a person's temperament, interactions with others, concern with making an impression, and effort put into achieving his or her goals.

Emotional Marks Dark dots that look like pepper. When scattered across the upper lip, they indicate that something is irritating the person or rubbing the individual the wrong way.

Energy Lines Dark lines, located on the outer and inner edges of a person's lip prints. They indicate where and how strongly a person's energies are focused.

Fingers of God Strong spiritual energy force, revealed by the presence of vertical white lines on the outside edge of the person's lip prints. Some compare these lines to the rays of sun, called Fingers of God, that are seen shining through clouds onto the water.

Fullness Plumpness of upper and lower lips of a print, from thin to wide; reveals a person's communication skills, thoroughness, frugality, analytical ability, and mathematical skills.

Gale Mark Vertical white lines(s) through upper or lower lip; signifies the person is going through a difficult situation, which could involve the loss of or separation from a loved one.

Gerbil Wheels Scattered white lines inside the upper and/or lower lips; reflect a lot of mental activity and a need to write things down.

Ghost Lips Light color on both upper and lower lips; reveal that the person is extremely tired.

Godfather and **Godmother** Square- or rectangle-shape lip prints; indicates a person well-grounded in his or her beliefs and firm in what he or she will and will not do.

Go-To Person One with square- or rectangle-shape lip print; solid and reliable person; the one to go to for help in solving problems.

Gourmet Lip Split Located on the inner edge at center of the lower lip; can be anything from an extreme V indentation to a slight one to none at all; reflects a person's eating preferences, sense of humor, and how romantic and sentimental he or she is.

Gut Mark Like an inverted V on the left or right outer edge of the lower lip; indicates the person needs to pay attention to his or her gut feelings when making a decision (also called Old Soul Mark).

Health Marks Dark dots that look like black pepper or smudges. When scattered across a person's lower lip, they indicate a need for attention to health issues.

Hug Pucker, Lower Lip An oblong shape on the lower inside edge that looks like a little hotdog or mushroom rising toward the upper lip; has to do with how people treat themselves and how confident they are.

Hug Pucker, Upper Lip An oblong shape on the upper inside edge that looks like a little hanging hotdog or mushroom; reveals information about the way people show affection and how much affection they want or need.

Incher Person whose lip prints have a narrow space between the upper and lower lip that increases only a little with each additional lip print made in succession; indicates the person does not make any sudden moves, and his or her comfort level has to be satisfied with each small move forward.

Information Funnel A V shape, located on the lip print corners; reveals that the person needs lots of information to make decisions.

Injury/Trauma Mark Missing outer edge of either the upper or lower lips; indicates that some part of the person's body needs attention. Upper lip concerns the upper body, and the lower lip concerns the lower body.

Juggler Medium-size lip print; indicates the person is able to handle many projects successfully.

Keepers People who reciprocate exceptional kindness and friendship and make wonderful lifelong friends.

Lip Print within a Lip Print A very lucky sign that says the person is almost always blessed with an extra boost of energy when needed and makes an excellent friend (but is also difficult to get close to).

Lipsologist One who practices Lipsology.

Lipsology The art and science of reading lip prints.

Mother Nature Lines Vertical white lines on the outside edge of the lower lip; indicate that it is important for the person to get outside for well-being and athletic ability.

Mr. or Ms. Stretch Marks People with Energy Lines on the outer edge on both the upper and lower lips of their lip print. They are stretched to the max!

Old Soul Mark Like an inverted V shape on the left or right outer edge of the lower lip; reveals the person is very intuitive and has true wisdom to share with others (also called Gut Mark).

Patters People with round- or oval-shaped lip prints. They pat people on the back and like things to go smoothly and for everyone to be happy.

Position of Prints on Paper Placement of lip print(s) relative to three columns, three rows, and nine individual zones on the paper. Each area represents a different relationship to timing, thinking, reality, and comfort levels.

Pushing Bar Like a little sausage or mushroom on the outer edge of the upper or lower lip; has to do with setting high goals.

Row One of three horizontal positions on the paper where a person made his or her lip prints; top, middle, and bottom representing the person's relationships to timing, thinking, reality, and comfort levels.

Seeds of Change White dots or small lines (seeds and/or grains), located in the body of the lower lip. They indicate that the person will do things that help lots of people in a positive way.

Shape The overall look of the outside perimeter of the lip print; indicates how successful a person is and in what ways.

Size The overall height and width of the lip print; demonstrates how a person tackles projects.

Spacing between Upper and Lower Lip Gap between upper and lower lips of a lip print; indicates the person's open-mindedness, commitment to projects, stubbornness, and how adventurous he or she is.

Spiritual Lines Vertical white lines on the outside edge of the upper lip; mean the person has a strong spiritual connection.

Starburst White dot located in the upper lip; signifies a person with positive, up-beat energy. Seeing this person brings a smile to others' lips.

Stress Lines Vertical white lines that start on the lips' inner edges and may go all the way through; also can appear as horizontal white lines across the upper and lower lips. Depending on their position, they indicate drained energy and dealing with stress, disappointment, and difficult situations.

Talent Scouts People with triangle-shaped lip prints. They have a gift of spotting talent in others and their lip prints want them to share that gift often.

Zingers Sharp or blunt protrusions from the corners of the lips; indicate a person speaks his or her mind.

Zone One of nine positions on the paper where a person made his or her lip prints. Each zone individually combines the meanings of the placement in the print's column and row positions, telling a person's story one lip print at a time.

BIBLIOGRAHY

Byrd, Anita. *Handwriting Analysis: A Guide to Personality.* New York: Arco Publishing, Inc., 1982.

Cheiro, *Palmistry for All.* New York: G. P. Putnam's Sons, 1916.

Eddy, Jilly. *Lipsology: The Art and Science of Reading Lip Prints, A Training Manual.* Bothell, Washington: Book Publishers Network, 2011.

Gardini, Maria. *The Secrets of the Hand.* New York: Macmillan Publishing Company, 1985.

Jensen, Bernard. *The Science and Practice of Iridology.* Provo, Utah: Bi World Publishers, Inc., 1952.

Levine, Roz. *Palmistry: How to Chart the Lines of Your Destiny.* New York: Fireside Simon & Shuster, 1992.

Lin, Henry. *What Your Face Reveals: Chinese Secrets of Face Reading.* Saint Paul, Minnesota: Llewellyn Publications, 1999.

Merton, Holmes. *Descriptive Mentality from the Head, Face, and Hand.* Philadelphia: David McKay Publisher, 1899.

O'Connell, Sheldon. *Hollywood Lip Prints: The Clay Campbell Collection.* Winona, Minnesota: Ironwood Press, Inc., 1989.

Reid, Lori. *The Art of Hand Reading,* New York: DK Publishing, 1999.

Rosetree, Laura. *I Can Read Your Face.* New York: Dell Publishing, 1990.

Rosetree, Rose. *Wrinkles Are God's Makeup: How You Can Find Meaning in Your Evolving Face.* Sterling, Virginia: Women's Intuition World Wide, LLC, 2003.

Sarno, John. *Healing Back Pain: The Mind-Body Connection*. New York: Grand Central Life and Style, 2010.

Weidenfeld. *With Love From ... A Collection of Celebrity Lipographs*. New York: A & W Publishers, Inc., 1980.

Tao, Li. *How to Read Faces*. New York: Crescent Books, 1986.

Tickle, Naomi R. *You Can Read a Face Like a Book: How Reading Faces Helps You Succeed in Business and Relationships*. Bishop, California: Daniels Publishing, 2003.

Whiteside, Robert. *Face Language*. New York: Pocket Books, 1975.

Young, Lailan. *Secrets of the Face: The Chinese Art of Reading Character from Faces*. London: Coronet Books, 1984.

INDEX

horizontal white lines on lips. *See* Stress Lines

Hug Pucker, lower lip (oblong shape center inside edge), 89–90
about lower lip Hug Puckers, 89, 157
moderate/slight, 90

Hug Pucker, upper lip (oblong shape center inside edge), 81–87
about upper lip Hug Puckers, 81, 157
children's prints, 82
extreme, 82
moderate, 83
none, 85
recessive, 86
slight, 84
stories about, 7–8
Stress Lines in, 81, 87 (*see also* Stress Lines)

identifying and interpreting prints, 17–24
identifying prints, 17–19
indecision when interpreting, 18–19
interpreting prints, 20–22
lip map, 23–24
new or unknown markings, 18–19
upper and lower lips, 24

Inchers and space between lips, 120, 157

indented V shape on inner edge at center of lower lip. *See* Gourmet Lip Split

indented V shape on outer edge at center of upper lip. *See* Cupid's Bow, upper lip

Information Funnels (V shapes on corners)
about Information Funnels, 98, 157
V shape, 108
V shape with Energy Lines, 109

Injury/Trauma Mark (missing outer edge)
about Injury/Trauma Marks, 157
on lower lip, 137
on upper lip, 128

intensity of color. *See* Color Intensity of lips

inverted V shape on outer edge at center of lower lip. *See* Cupid's Bow, lower lip

Jilly Eddy and lipsology
Certified Lipsologists, ix, 5, 153, 155
history of lipsology, 3–6
how lipsology works, 7–9
lipsologist, defined, 158
true spirit of lipsology, 10–11
website, 153

Juggler, lip size of, 29, 157

Keepers and Energy Lines, 53, 157

large size of lips, 27–28
light color of lips, 42–43
lighter color in lower lip than in upper lip, 45
lighter color in upper lip than in lower lip, 44

Lipsology: The Art and Science of Reading Lip Prints

triangle shape of lips, 31, 34
true spirit of lipsology, 10–11
unknown markings, identifying,
18–19
upper lip fullness. *See* Fullness
of lips
upper lip generally, 24

V shapes
Angel Mark (V shape on outer
edge of upper lip), 124–
125
indention on center inner
edge of lower lip (*see*
Gourmet Lip Split)
indention on center outer
edge of upper lip (*see*
Cupid's Bow, upper lip)
inverted V shape on outer
edge at center of lower
lip (*see* Cupid's Bow,
lower lip)
Old Soul or Gut Mark
(inverted V on outer
edge of lower lip), 139
V shapes on corners (*see*
Information Funnels)
variation in lip prints, 17–18
vertical white line or lines
through upper or lower
lip. *See* Gale Mark
vertical white lines on inner
edges. *See* Stress Lines
vertical white lines on outer
edge of lower lip. *See*
Mother Nature Lines
vertical white lines on outer
edge of upper lip. *See*
Spiritual Lines

wavy shape of lips, 31, 37
website, lipsology, 153
white dot on upper lip
(Starburst), 131, 159
white dots or small lines
on lower lip (Seeds of
Change), 140, 159
white lines, scattered. *See*
Gerbil Wheels
white lines, vertical, on outer
edge of lower lip (Mother
Nature Lines), 138, 158
white lines, vertical, on
outer edge of upper lip
(Spiritual Lines), 129–130,
159
*With Love from ... A Collection
of Celebrity Lipographs*, 3

Zingers (blunt to sharp
protrusion on corners)
about Zingers, 110, 159
comparison with Angel
Wings, 98, 111
in corners, 98, 110
on round/oval lips, 36
zones of lip prints on paper.
See Position of Lip Prints
on Paper